The
Stories That Shocked
The Islands

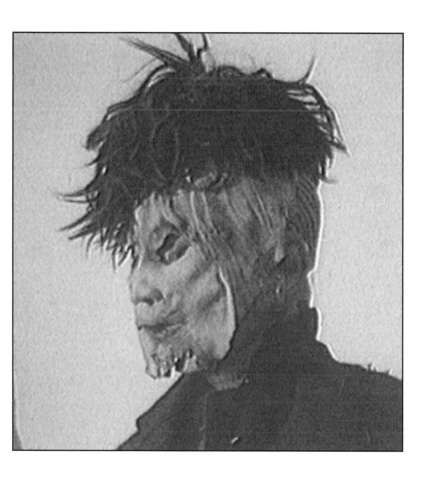

The
Stories That Shocked
The Islands

Channel Island Publishing
www.channelislandpublishing.com

Written by Samantha Bourgeois
Published in 2007 by
Channel Island Publishing
Unit 3b, Barette Commercial Centre
La Route du Mont Mado
St John, Jersey JE3 4DS

CHANNEL
ISLAND
PUBLISHING

We acknowledge with thanks permission to reproduce
photographs supplied by various sources including:
Channel Television
Axiom Design
Guernsey Museum Service
Michael Holmes
Richard Weithley
Stuart Abraham
Gary Grimshaw
Sally Bardin
Michael Ginns M.B.E
Mr & Mrs Tredant
Publishers own collection
Printed by Cromwell Press, Trowbridge, Wiltshire

ISBN 1-905095-15-5

CONTENTS

TV detective Jim Bergerac in front of Jersey's most famous landmark, Gorey Cas[

Introduction

The Channel Islands are famous all around the globe, which is surprising considering their small land-mass and population. An American State was even named after Jersey, being called 'New Jersey' in 1650.

Whether it's the famous Jersey cow, which has been exported to every corner of the world, the Jersey and Guernsey sweaters of yesteryear, or the 'Jersey Royal' potato and the Guernsey tomato, the Islands seem to have spread their influence far and wide.

During World War II the Channel Islands were the only part of Britain to be occupied by the Germans, which created much media interest after the war. Then, of course, there was TV detective Jim Bergerac who in the 1980s put Jersey firmly on the map. Nowadays it is the Islands' role as international finance centres that seems to be constantly in the spotlight. But these are not the only reasons why the eyes of the world have turned to our Islands, as you will read in this book. All the stories related here have one thing in common: they were all shocking in their time and would have been major topics of conversation in the Islands, as well as hitting the local, national or international headlines.

The stories cover a broad spectrum, from tales of witch-trials in the seventeenth century to shipwrecks in the twenty-first. Some are amusing, some have happy endings, some are simply curious, and others are tragic. Hopefully there is enough of a cross-section to give you a good idea of some of the extraordinary events that these small Islands have witnessed over the years.

As time passes and the present becomes history, many of the day-to-day happenings fade away. What shocks us today may be forgotten entirely by future generations. Here we record some 'lest we forget' and look back at the stories that shocked the Islands at various times in their history.

If these tales whet your appetite, then rest assured that there are plenty more in the archives and we hope to include others in future editions.

Chapter One

Witchcraft and Legends

W hat do we mean when we talk about a 'witch'? Children's fairy tales, spooky television programmes and good old ghost stories which are told on school trips all help to reinforce the same image in our mind. A witch, in the stereotypical sense, would be an old woman sitting astride a broom, wearing a pointy hat and cackling an evil laugh. She would have a large nose with warts on it - and of course she would have a black cat. You can see much the same costume worn by little girls on All Hallows Eve (Hallowe'en), the main calendar date for witches to be out and about. An official definition of a witch is a woman who professes, or is believed, to practice magic - that's black magic or the 'black art'. In other words, she is a sorceress.

This is the story of our Island's involvement with witchcraft and the legends that keep the stories brewing. It all occurred during the sixteenth and seventeenth centuries, when rumours of witches rapidly caused widespread concern throughout Europe, including the Channel Islands. There are a few theories as to why these witches arose. Firstly it was believed that the Catholic Church had tried, but failed, to wipe out Pagan beliefs, instead simply driving them underground and causing their religion to become a 'secret society'. Anyone who had tokens of Paganism including symbols, books, or rituals were made to renounce them. Unless people observed the strict codes of Calvinism, they would have been seen to be a devil worshipper and therefore an enemy of God. This does not mean, however, that these people were all witches - it might be simply that they followed other religions. Another theory was that devil-worship was one of many religious doctrines to have become immensely popular.

Between 1550 and 1661 at least 85 Islanders were condemned as witches, put through a trial and died at the stake. Being a witch was a crime, and just as you could have been arrested for theft or assault, if people called you a witch you were arrested immediately. Most of the time the people arrested were not witches at all, but they were probably thought of as odd, or immoral, or overly superstitious. Perhaps they were just 'different' or were outsiders. These were victims of the Island's law which was created in the belief that the devil and his disciples lived here.

How would you protect yourself from something you were scared of and knew nothing about? Well back then it was believed that if you hung or engraved crosses over the doors of your house and other entrances, such as windows and chimneys, it would warn off evil spirits and curses. By carrying an acorn in your pocket, you could guard against evil. Superstition or not, this would help to put people's minds at ease. Many people did admit to seeing the devil and confessed to having an 'evil eye' which meant they could cause damage and harm to their neighbours. They were said to be able to put a curse on someone so that they would sicken and die, and many so-called witches claimed they had cursed a farmer's land and animals. With farming being of such importance to the Island, it was easy to blame witchcraft when animals died or crops failed. As in children's stories, you can imagine members of the community seeking out the person who had been named as a witch, walking with stakes and pick-axes by fire-light, and shouting 'witch, witch, witch'. This is exactly what the people of these Islands did. It was a case of seek and destroy.

Later on, Jersey settled these disputes by what it called 'The Judgement of God', with cross, water and fire. The first step was for the accused to stand in a position that resembled a cross. Whoever stood there the longest was seen to be one of God's own and not a witch. The second step was really cruel, as it consisted of boiling a cauldron of water and placing a weight inside it. To prove their innocence the accused had to put their bare hands into the water to collect the weight, then carry it whatever distance had been set. This wasn't the end of their torture: they then had their hand wrapped with the weight still in it, and had to keep it like that for three days. Once released from this excruciating pain, if their hands were not scalded they were declared innocent. This was a brutal test as it is impossible to come away without any type of mark or burn. The third step, 'fire', used the same method as the second, but this time with a red-hot iron. Any innocent defendant would not have stood a chance because, once they were tarnished with being named as a witch, they were tricked and bullied until they eventually gave up. There was never any form of prison sentence once you were declared a witch; death was always on the cards. A condemned man or woman was ordered to leave the courtroom with a rope around their neck, and go straight to their execution at the marketplace (this is where the Royal Square is today.) But it did not even stop at death: the body was then taken away to be burnt until nothing but ashes was left.

To this day no-one is certain how witchcraft came to the Islands. Perhaps when Pagans had their beliefs taken from them, some turned to witchcraft? Or perhaps it was simply about superstition and the chance for some 'amusement' in using inhuman methods to drive out evil? It wasn't until 1692 that witch trials ceased. You can read about the trials in documented confessions and court reports. It has been recorded that for every square mile of the Channel Islands at least one Islander was whipped, tortured, banished or executed. There are many sites around Jersey where there is evidence of these tales, mainly around the dolmens - the standing stones that were apparently used by Neolithic man for religious ceremonies. One of these, the Faldouet dolmen, was even exorcised twice, in 1981 and 1982, because witnesses had seen and heard unusual activities. There are also many burial chambers throughout the Island. Witchcraft is not as frightening as it once used to be. Teenagers on the Island have been known to attempt 'spells' and make 'potions.' But this may be just part of the Gothic fashion culture and the belief that practising and indulging in the world of the black arts will not bring any repercussions. Many of us have read or seen something about witchcraft and most of the time we have the sense not to participate, or have been warned off by others. If you are a believer you know to 'handle with care' and if you don't, then the best thing would be not to take part - especially if you are not sure what you are getting yourself into.

In this 1568 drawing a 'Witch' is getting married to the Devil

Jersey is the biggest of the Channel Islands, and probably for that reason it had the lion's share of the witchcraft stories. The other Islands were not excluded however. In Guernsey the people were just as scared by the thought of satanic rituals being held on the Island. Between 1550 and 1661, some 54 people were burned at the stake in Guernsey, 32 executed in Jersey and 36 banished from the Islands. At Beaugard Tower near St Peter Port, they interrogated prisoners in a very inhumane way. They used a hand-cranked machine called a 'strappado.' It was very large and clumsily built. It was used to tear out the victims' limbs. Questions were asked by the persecutor, who then wrote down the answers. As you could imagine, the pain must have been intolerable, so many pleaded guilty even if they had been innocent.

*

Bad Books of Guernsey

Witchcraft in Guernsey was very secretive because the main form of this sorcery was based on a set of indestructible books also known as 'Les mauvais livres,' meaning bad books. The books were used to invoke demons, and the most well-known of these were the Albert books which contained recipes for spells and incantations. As to be expected, many people denied owning a copy. They were very small books written in French. In the nineteenth century over 400,000 copies of the book were printed and sold, which made it one of the best-sellers of the century. The books were cheaply made; some just sewn together with string. It was also said that these were republished all around the world including America. It was Guernsey which had the worst reputation for their use. These books provided chants and pictures for whoever wanted to cast spells: some were sick and ghastly, such as how to abort a child.

Others had a more humourous value, which we are able to laugh about now. One story is of an old lady who was angry with her neighbour and went out seeking revenge. She placed a curse upon the unsuspecting neighbour, which made him walk and walk all the way around the Island until she decided to lift the curse. Whether she did or not is again a mystery: you never know, you might just bump into him. On the more serious side, many people were so petrified that the mere mention of the books caused them to lose all colour in their faces. People genuinely believed that the misfortunes that happened to them were caused by the books. If you were to translate the exact meaning of the words, some chants were simply 'wing of bat and eye of newt'. Again, we may laugh at the ridiculous nature of these books, but even today many of the older generation of Guernsey are still frightened.

The 'mauvais livres' were considered indestructible: even when people try to get rid of them by burning them or throwing them into the sea, they would re-appear in their original place. It was said that the only way to get rid of these books was by burying them in a grave, then drenching the area with holy water while reciting a service of the Lord. Copies still exist today and some can be found in the Guille-Alles Library.

Alderney had few witches, but records show that there were four people who were sent to live in Guernsey because they had been accused of practising witchcraft and other forms of black magic. The four people were all French and in those days anyone who appeared different, or to have been seen as an outsider, would have been mistrusted. Firstly in 1620 Jean Behout and Girette Parmentier were banished from the entire Channel Islands. In 1634, almost 15 years later, Jacob

Gauddion was the next to be banished. Unfortunately for the fourth person she never made it off the Islands. On 3 May 1639 Emei Fleres was burnt on the gibbets.

*

Legends

Because the Channel Islands are steeped in such history it is easy to see how some ghostly stories have become the folklore that they are today. Whether it be the ghost of Lillie Langtry at the Opera House or the soldiers of the Jersey War Tunnels or Whitegates in Alderney there seems to be a chilling story at every turn. These stories re-appear year after year and, with the help of our imaginations, we create some of the most spectacular legends of today. Some of the most beautiful places on Jersey, Guernsey and the other Channel Islands are the spookiest places at night. The wonderful pathways where we like to take an afternoon stroll, the cliff tops where we gaze at the fabulous views, and even the beautiful tree-filled woods and lanes are the places of strange happenings. Here are just some of the things that might be watching you.

Black Dog of Bouley Bay

The Black Dog of Bouley Bay is a legend known through out the Island. It is a story that has been passed through generations to become the legend it is today. The 'Black Dog' itself has been described as a giant creature with yellow eyes as big as saucers and long sharp teeth.

Today a bar in Bouley Bay is named after the Legend

15

It patrols the beaches and cliff paths at night dragging its chains behind it, looking for its next foolish victim. Eyewitnesses of an encounter said that they had heard the sound of chains which terrified them to the point of freezing them to the spot. The dog would then circle the victim getting faster and faster each time. People have been found cowering in bushes scared of what they might have seen, clinging onto branches in a state of shock. Though there were never many face-to-face encounters, people often reported the clanging of what was thought were the chains being dragged along. On hearing this people would vacate the area immediately.

There are no records to be found of any victim having injuries which could have been caused by a vicious dog attack and it is rumoured that the beast was dreamt up by fishermen in order to keep people away from the bay so that they could get on with their illegal activities, such as smuggling brandy and tobacco. One infamous fisherman was Franique Desclios who lived alone in a small cottage at the foot of Bouley Bay but who had drowned in the harbour. Because of the size of his home, his coffin was laid out in the office of the undertakers. On the day of his funeral he was visited by many, including his fishermen friends. The undertaker had set up two coffins in his office and, to the astonishment of Franique's friends, it was discovered that that they had taken the wrong coffin to bury. At this point a rumour circulated, saying that there had been a sighting of the Black Dog near the church and in panic people evacuated the area. Unknown to everyone else at the time; Franique's fellow smugglers then dug up the grave with their spades, and retrieved their coffin - it was full of contraband. Later they gave their good friend Franique a belated funeral - all with help from the 'black dog'.

Nowadays people are less likely to worry about the Black Dog, which could be due to the laws and regulations being so tight, (if you believe the smugglers story). If the Black Dog really existed or is still around to this day, it is said if you see him near Bouley Bay that a storm is a-brewing.

*

The Werewolves of Forest, Guernsey

Many stories that are told today are for our entertainment, but in years gone by many were told by the elder of the family as a warning to its younger members. This was to ensure they would not go wandering off in dangerous places.

Similar to the story of Jersey's Black Dog, Guernsey was said to have a group of very vicious werewolves. Whereas on Jersey smuggling was a well-kept secret, it was known that there was smuggling going on around the Forest lanes of Guernsey and that in fact these so-called werewolves were employed by the smugglers. The smugglers hired men who needed to escape the duty of the Crown and dressed them up to resemble werewolves. Being paid only in food and drink, they took their job very seriously. They were used as a distraction so the smugglers could get on with their business without hassle. The local churches gave out warnings, telling people not to hang around the Forest lanes as they were not safe. With the Black Dog of Jersey being the figment of people's imaginations and superstious nature, the werewolves of Guernsey were real men. They enjoyed frightening the locals, and even began entering many people's houses and committing assaults. I believe that they lost themselves in their role of playing a werewolf, as they even used to gather together under thorn bushes on stormy nights. These tales have been handed down through the generations from the unfortunate people who had, more than likely, disturbed these werewolves at their work.

The Bride of St Lawrence

There are many spooky tales that revolve around the parish of St Lawrence: even the emblem on the shield is of the grid on which St Lawrence himself was roasted alive on, which to me seems slightly morbid.

The most well-known story that is still spoken of today is of the bride of St Lawrence. Many people are frightened of the Waterworks valley area because of the ghostly and harrowing atmosphere. It all began when a young woman, preparing herself to be wed, dressed in a beautiful white gown and came through the valley in her coach; being pulled by two bright white horses. She was excited to be marrying the man she so loved. On arriving at the church she was met by friends who told her that the bridegroom had never arrived. Distraught and shocked, she asked the coachmen to take her home. Later that night the lonely young woman, in despair at having been rejected, committed suicide. In those days marrying a man was very important to a woman as, unlike today, a woman's main role was to be a good home-maker and to raise a family. For this to have happened to the young woman would have caused her humiliation throughout the community. How the story continues is the creepy part. It is said that once a year at exactly midnight, she still rides down to the church following the sound of the bells. On the coachman's whip there are white ribbons attached, and the young woman is dressed in the same wedding dress she wore all those years ago. Onlookers have stated that when they have encountered this ghostly figure, the bride has no face, and her white bridal veil is draped around her grinning skull. It was hard to put a date to this harrowing tale, so how long ago it occurred is a mystery to me. However, I am not one to assume this is only a story, just in case one night I find myself strolling alone around Waterworks valley.

A Mother's Tragedy

On the Island of Guernsey it seems that most of its ghostly tales concern the same area, which is St Peter Port. On the steps of Tower Hill many locals have had sightings of a silhouette of an old women floating. People believe that this could be linked to the death of a mother and her two daughters in 1556. Katherine Cawehes and her two daughters Guillemine Gibert and Perotine Massey were all reported to the dean for not attending church. With no time for forgiveness, their pleas were refused and they were burned alive at the stake for being Witches. A ghastly twist which is believed to have occurred is that one of the daughters was heavily pregnant, and gave birth there and then. People looked on in horror, then someone reached in and took the new-born baby out of the fire. The Bailiff turned around and threw the baby back onto the fire, as he was adamant that he was to dispose of anything that would remind them of that family. If you go to the top of Tower Hill steps, you will be able to see a plaque which has been erected in remembrance of the mother and her daughters. Many people who have supposedly seen the ghost of the burned women have been so scared that they insist on remaining anonymous when they talk about their experience.

An etching from that time showing the baby and the horrendous event

Geffroy's Leap

Even though there haven't been any ghostly sightings of Geffroy many people are infatuated with the story of Geffroy's Leap because there are so many tales attached to it. This could have been caused through simple Chinese whispers throughout the years. The truth behind the legend is unsure (and no-one really knows whether Geffroy actually existed), but many simply choose to tell the story of which they are most fond.

The site of Geffroy's Leap, also known as Le Saut Geffroy, is situated between Gorey Castle and Anne Port Bay in the parish of St Martin.

The first of the stories is that Geffroy had been a prisoner in the castle. One night he managed to make his escape, but was then chased by the soldiers all the way around the cliff edge. Before they were able to catch him he jumped straight off the cliff, narrowly missing the rocks and swimming straight to shore. He was easily recaptured. The guards and the bystanders were completely bewildered as to how he'd managed to survive, and an officer then gave Geffroy an ultimatum. He now had the choice either to go back to prison or to have his freedom: if he could perform this miraculous stunt again, he would go free. Like anyone in the situation of having to do a prison sentence, he literally jumped at the chance. However this time, without realising the tide had been going out; he jumped, landed on the rocks and died on impact.

The second of the stories is one with more passion and many have seen it to be an unusual love story. What is said to have happened is that Geffroy was convicted of a crime against a woman. He was quite well known around the area, with a reputation of being flirtatious with younger women and apparently this time he took it too far. He was sentenced to death, and on the appointed hour two pallbearers and a masked executioner led Geffroy to the edge of the cliff, where he was pushed off to his death. Many of the onlookers were women, mainly seeking justice. As in the other story he survived, much to everyone's astonishment, and swam ashore at Anne Port. Some then believed that this proved his innocence. With mothers annoyed that he had survived and daughters smiling in delight, he willingly - though a bit hastily - stepped forward and offered to jump again. Of course the second jump was fatal and it is said that when he died he did not only break his neck, but the hearts of many young women as well. Neither version of the story has any facts to back it up, but both are great tales to keep passing down through generations as part of Jersey's culture and heritage. Geffroy's Leap is now preserved by the National Trust for Jersey.

Chapter Two

All at Sea

As you would expect in small Island communities the sea and sailing upon it has always played a major part of day-to-day life in the Islands. Inevitably then the stories of tragedy at sea are unfortunately almost common place.

The Channel Islands are known for their beautiful beaches and luscious views. But how much do we really know about what rests on the seabed beneath the waves? Many ships, from as far back as Roman times right through to the twenty first century, have been wrecked and sunk off the coasts of Jersey, Guernsey and Alderney. They include passenger ships, cargo vessels and warships. Through logs, reports, investigations by archaeologists, and stories told by the survivors, we know a great deal about them. We are also fortunate to have pictures and other visual evidence thanks to the efforts of the divers like John Ovenden who have been trying to preserve the wrecks in their original state. Some wrecks have now been registered, which means that divers are not able to take any little treasures they might find. Amazingly many of the shipwrecks are in good condition - still in one piece to the extent that you can make out which parts are which. Recording them is a very good idea as it helps to keep the heritage of the Islands alive.

Many of the ships that came to grief off the coasts of the Islands did so because of our shallow sea and the sharply pointed rocks that protrude from it. The deepest waters lie to the west of the Islands at around 80 meters (260 feet). However in most parts the sea can be as shallow as 20 meters (66 feet). That doesn't sound particularly shallow if you see it through a swimmer's eyes, but when you're a heavy ship carrying cargo as well as passengers, then it's a different story altogether. In spring the tides are at their highest and lowest, and it is at a low spring tides when navigating around the Islands is particularly treacherous. Between Jersey and France, and between Herm and Alderney, there is said to be a continuous stream of shoal and rock. Another amazing thing about Jersey is that it has the highest tides and fastest currents in the whole of Europe. Indeed, Jersey and the other Channel Islands have some of the most dangerous waters in the Northern Hemisphere. When the fog is thick and you are being pushed along by a strong wind, it makes the waters very unpleasant to sail through.

In 1962 a maritime historian named John David reported that 392 vessels were wrecked off Guernsey, Alderney and Sark between 1278 and 1962. If that total had included Jersey as well it would have no doubt run into many more hundreds, not to mention the more recent wrecks such as the Radiant Med in 1984 and the levoli Sun in 2000.

Against the background of the Islands' rich history, tales of the shipwrecks are always fascinating, but it's important not to forget the human aspect - the lives that were dramatically affected by these disasters. Hundreds, maybe thousands, died, and many passengers and crew were seriously injured. On board the warships were men who were risking their lives for us, and many more Islanders took equal risks in order to rescue people from ships that were in trouble.

Here we take a look at just two of these shipwrecks, both of which happened around Easter weekend, but whose stories are nearly 100 years apart.

The Stella - 1899 (Titanic of the Channel Islands)

Everyone has heard the tragic tale about The*Titanic* sinking on her maiden voyage. It's a famous story which has hit the Hollywood screens on a number of occasions. But how many of us today know about the *Stella?* It was a steamship belonging to London and South Western Railway and was thought to have smashed, in thick fog and at high speed, into the infamous Casquets reef seven miles off Alderney. There have been many theories as to why, how, and who was to blame for this disaster in which 77 passengers and crew members lost their lives.

At the time steam-driven ships were a Godsend, seen as the beginning of a new era for the Channel Islands. The vessels were all about speed, comfort and new technology. They may seem primitive to us today because this was an era before the invention of radar or satellite navigation systems. Radio transmitters were not often used, and not every vessel even had access to Morse code transmitters. The main purpose of these powerful ships was to carry passengers, but they also had to deliver the mail. Speed was vital if they were to beat their competitors, so passenger safety might not have been at the top of their agenda.

On Thursday 30 March 1899, London and South Western Railway ran their very first daylight mail service of the season to the Channel Islands. The company's train left London with 110 passengers and arrived just after 11am at Southampton, where an extra 37 passengers met at the dock and boarded the *Stella*. It was a warm, sunny day. People were either travelling home or were off on their holidays for Easter. The *Stella* left at 11.25am - already ten minutes late - and steamed towards the Casquets. It was a calm sea with a slight swell and a chilly breeze.

There were originally three lighthouses on the Casquets reef, but two of these coal-burning lights had been destroyed by a huge storm in 1823 and not replaced. As the *Stella* approached, therefore, the Casquets reef was guarded by just one lighthouse. This stood over 120 feet above the water, with a bright glowing light that flashed three times every 30 seconds. In dense fog, the light would have been of little use, but there was also a horn-blower to warn sailors of the fog and of the reef.

The *Stella* was under the command of Captain William Reeks. Throughout his career he had commanded many other ships, some regularly shipping from Southampton to Jersey. He was a well-respected captain and took pride in his work. He must also have been proud to be at the helm of the *Stella,* a handsome ship that had been built in Glasgow and launched in October 1890, with its first trip on the 16 November. No expense had been spared in fitting out the *Stella:* it had large brass skylights and rich wooden furniture, and was one of the first ships on the route to have electric light. It had a superb galley, where hot meals were prepared for all the passengers, and a comfortable dining saloon covered in elegant floral tiles. In fact, the ship was beautiful all the way down to the minor details such as the crockery, with the plates, cups and saucers all featuring the emblems of the Royal Mail and the London and South Western Railway.

The *Stella* was 253 feet in length, 35 feet in the main and 15 feet deep, weighing in at about 1,059 tons - a big vessel for around that time. Its top speed was around 19 knots. Considering that it was used for delivering mail as well as passengers, it was very long and elegant in a yacht shape.

The *Stella*'s single funnel was painted cream and was fitted with the technology wonders of that time. At 1pm Captain Reeks went to have lunch with the passengers. He saw no problem with the weather as it was still calm and sunny, so he continued to sail close to the top speed (around 18 and a half knots.) A little before 3pm a haze began to form a white blanket over the blue sky. Captain Reeks made the command for the *Stella* to slow down. It slowed to 12 knots, continuously sounding the horn. After 10 minutes, the mist began to lift slightly and the Captain ordered it back to full speed. As master of the ship, he had two means of checking its progress, a spinner which helped to check the distance travelled, and the log. Neither navigation was accurate. By 3.30pm the fog had thickened so much that visibility dropped enormously.

Captain Reeks sent a seaman to the bow of the ship to look out for any oncoming hazards and to listen for foghorns. At this point Reeks estimated that the ship was at least 40 minutes away from the Casquets. The *Stella* was still at full speed with her whistle blowing. At 3.55pm the chief engineer rang up another interval. The vessel was closing in very fast to the reef. No-one had heard the foghorn. By 4pm they eventually heard the loud blast. Men who were standing on the bridge had thought that they had seen an opening, but all of a sudden an immense rock came out from nowhere. The *Stella* stood no chance: at full speed the ship needed at least a quarter of a mile to stop. She was within 12 seconds of the reef and all 1,059 tons of the ship at 18 knots or nearly 21 miles an hour scraped over the reef. Passengers were flung from their bunks. Within seconds of the impact the engine-room was filled ankle-deep in water. It would be only minutes until the boat was fully submerged.

The captain ordered women and children to be put on the lifeboats first, followed by the men. A few went with the women and children but these were mainly seamen and crew: the rest waited until the end. There was no shortage of life-jackets, with more than 700 on board, but getting everyone into the lifeboats was another matter. One female crew-member, Mary Anne Rogers, gave up her life jacket and seat on the lifeboat to another woman. Even though this was an heroic and brave thing to do it ended in another life being lost - hers.

It has been said that if the crew and passengers had realised just how quickly the ship would sink, then the death toll could have been cut in half. At one point everything seemed to be going quite calmly, but once the realisation set in as to how fast the ship was sinking passengers started to panic. They began to leap over the ship's railings and cling for dear life onto bits of wood or anything they could find that might keep them afloat. The air temperature was below freezing and the water was bitterly cold. Many died because they froze to death, others drowned. In the *Stella*'s final plunge lifeboats were still being boarded. The only crew-member on the bridge to survive was George Reynolds.

In a very short space of time, five lifeboats had been launched, showing remarkable courage and seamanship from the crew and helpers. The *Stella*'s bow lifted high into the sky, with great blasts of air continuing to bubble out. The Captain stayed aboard, and was said to have stood with his arms in their air as the ship went down. It was a very honourable and worthy act and many might assume he did it not just because it was his duty but because he believed the wrecking of the *Stella* was his fault.

Captain Reeks had miscalculated on two counts. Firstly the ship had sailed too far east. Secondly the ship was further ahead by a few miles than anticipated. His inaccurate calculations were taken to the bottom of the sea with him. Because of this, enquiries had to be made and they had to do the best they could to reconstruct what must have happened.

One 14-year-old boy had a miraculous escape: he found a football on deck and attached it to the lapel of his coat, so that he would float in the water. His name was Bening Arnold. He survived the rest of the day, the whole of the next day, and part of the following day. Along with 12 other people, he clung to the upturned hull of a lifeboat. One by one, they died due to the cold, the shock and the pure exhaustion. By the time they were rescued, off the coast of Cherbourg, there were only three men alive with Bening. His mother and younger brother were not so lucky: they both drowned. In later years, Bening's son told stories about his father's experience and put his survival down to the fact that he was a strong swimmer, a bit of a tough boy, and was wearing thick Victorian clothes - as good as a wet-suit in terms of protection.

The extent of tragedy began to unfold as more survivors were picked up. Four lifeboats filled to the brim with passengers from the *Stella* were found and many had been adrift for 27 hours.

One of the theories about this accident started with London and South Western Railway services strongest competitor, the Great Western Railway another shipping company who also did the Channel Island run. On this day both companies had identical arrival times for Guernsey. It was believed that the captain of the *Stella* was racing the other vessel to ensure it reached Guernsey first. Is this the truth? They will never find out. The board of enquiry was unconvinced. They investigated the schedules, found no explanation and came to the obvious conclusion that ships' arrival times should be staggered. Captain Reeks was simply following his schedule and even though he had died, he had to take the full weight of blame. Clearly the ship's speed should have been reduced after 3.13pm and soundings made. This was the captain's mistake. One passenger stated that she saw rocks on either side of the vessel, which means that it was highly unlikely it struck the Noir Rock as suggested. The horn from the lighthouse would have been heard, making the vessel not far from the reef. If this had been the case then the passengers would have been able to climb up onto the rocks to safety. The *Stella* did not come to rest on the reefs then slip back into deep water. Its position suggests that she went right over the reefs and that the sudden stillness was a mere deception. The final death-plunge of the ship was over a kilometre away from where she had made contact with rocks. She may have been a large ship, but because of a lack of technology and knowledge, once sunk she simply went missing and no-one knew where she was. So the ship lay there at rest waiting for someone to discover her.

Asleep at the bottom of the seabed the *Stella* lay, gradually decomposing and becoming a new home for the fish and other sea life. The wreck was not found until 73 years later by local divers Richard Keen and Fred Shaw. Even then it was by accident because they were looking for a different ship. When they saw the wreck, they immediately realised it was the *Stella* and were very excited about their discovery. They were also amazed that it was in such good condition for the length of time it had been there. This is believed to be due to the fact that it had submerged to a depth of 55 metres.

Twenty-one years after this first discovery, a man named John Ovenden re-discovered the *Stella*. John had a movie-camera and was able to capture footage of the wreck. Now everyone could see what the lost ship looked like. People began taking little trinkets from the wreck as souvenirs which is all well and good, but over the four years that John had now been diving, most of the artifacts had gone and the historic wreck was disappearing before his very eyes. So John took it upon himself to save the *Stella* and managed to get it protected as a listed wreck. Both of the ship's propellers are with the wreck, showing that she fell well clear of the Casquets reef, as one propeller broke off and was found close to the ship.

Many artifacts have been discovered, including plates, toilets, shoes, and even a 95-year-old light bulb with the filament still intact. Some of the items are very exciting finds, such as the ship's log, which puts on record the moment in time and speed that the boat had been travelling in its fatal last minutes.

The loss of the *Stella* affected the whole of the Channel Islands. Because it was so close to home, everyone knew someone, or knew of someone, who was a passenger. Such a tragedy is long-lasting. Sadly, with an unblemished career under his belt, Captain William Reeks was blamed. A year after the tragedy of the *Stella*, the London and South Western Rail way service and their competitors, the Great Western Railway Service, changed the way they operated. Instead of advertisements promoting speed and commercial enterprise, they began promoting safety. The final death toll had been 77 women, men and children. Many families lost so much that year and should be remembered for their bravery. If only they had realised how important safety was the first time around.

The 'Stella' leaves St Helier Harbour in 1898, a year before the disaster

A sketch of the infamous Casquets

Channiland 1995

The 'St Malo', was part of the Channiland ferry line fleet, it was a regular high-speed ship with a regular route: a reliable, modern vessel that was not associated with accidents. Many ferries had sailed this route because it was a common commuting channel that took ships daily through the Channel Islands and on to France and back.

At 9.30am on 17th April 1995 the ship, which had come from its port in France, left Jersey and continued on its way through the English Channel heading to Guernsey. It was an Easter Monday and many people were on their way back home after a relaxing holiday.

It was very much a normal day. The weather was nice, the seas were calm apart from a few swells, and there seemed nothing to be concerned about. There didn't even seem to be much chance of getting seasick. The Jersey harbour-master Roy Bullen says that the coast of Jersey is not without its perils: with its strong currents and hidden dangers such as rocks, it is usually better for large ships to sail further out and give the Island a wide berth. On that day, however, Captain Phillippe Peneau decided to take a short cut and even though he knew he was off-course, he failed to slow down from over 32 knots or 37mph. Most people like to get home quickly after a holiday, but my mum always used to say something about it being better to be slow and steady - and she's got a point. A couple of passengers on board were regular travellers and they noticed that the St Malo was very close to the shore. It had only been at sea for around 20 minutes when there was a sudden violent crunch as the ship ploughed straight into a rock.

The sound of grating metal flowed through the ship and in that instant the boat lifted up and out of the water. Lights went out and for a few minutes it went very quiet. Passengers on board had no idea what was going on, and panic started to well up. No-one told them what was happening and they couldn't even find any of the seven crew members. What should they do? It wasn't until one passenger got his life-jacket from under his seat and placed it over his head that everyone else started to do the same thing.

The ferry began to fall onto its port side with the passenger windows being submerged under the water. There appeared to be a puncture through the floor, with the water gushing out like a shower-spray. By this time the passengers were all on the deck waiting to be rescued. The captain had announced the ship's distress as he sent out a mayday: "There is water rushing into gaping holes - the *St Malo* is sinking."

The ship had come to grief just off the coast of Corbière. The boat turned further and further onto its side and people feared they would drown. Eventually a crew-member appeared to lead the passengers to an evacuation point.

Life-rafts had been placed in the sea and were ready for the passengers to evacuate. Amid the swell of the sea, people were being thrown from one side to another. Even the elderly and disabled had to jump 15 feet into a life-raft and some even broke limbs on the impact of their fall. Everyone had to climb over railings in order to jump: there were ladders, which were supposed to help in an evacuation, but they proved too difficult and awkward to use. Once in a raft, each passenger had to crawl from one life-raft to another to enable the others behind them to land as safely as possible. Rescue ships had arrived but were struggling to get to them. Many of boats had heard the mayday and went on their way to help in the best way that they could: this included the Isle of Man Ferry commanded by Peter Falla which was on hire to Condor Ferries at the time. He arrived to find the ship sinking and was worried that if it was to sink it would take the life rafts down as well. He managed to manoeuvre his ship steadily alongside the *St Malo*, close enough to reach passengers. Keeping control took every ounce of his skills and training as a captain. The current could at any minute push him towards the life-rafts, crushing the passengers, or he might drift onto the rocks endangering his own passengers. Captain Peter Falla tried several times to approach the life-rafts and in one heart-stopping moment his ferry nearly crushed the life-rafts between the two ships. Finally he was able to manoeuvre his ship skillfully through the swell of the sea and his crew helped people aboard.

On land, harbour-master Roy Bullen was struggling to stay on top of things, as there was a problem with communication. Out at the scene of the accident the helicopters were disturbing any form of radio communication, making it hard to keep track of the many boats that had come to help. The crews of all the ships were aware that there were 300 passengers in need of rescue. Boats were doing the best they could as many people were in shock and were freezing cold or panicking. Some of the boats accidentally collided with the life-rafts, which made people very scared, some of them beginning to feel that they weren't going to make it. Eventually all passengers were rescued, though some had suffered serious injuries and had to be immediately air-lifted to hospital. Others were suffering from shock and minor injuries, they were also checked out at the hospital. Luckily for everyone, there were no fatalities and even the boat was towed to a nearby beach and saved.

Captain Peter Falla who was on the Isle of Man Ferry, was the last one to leave as he stayed to make sure everyone had made it safely back to the shore. It took the crew around 77 minutes to ensure that all passengers were safely off the boat, even though the recommended time is 30 minutes. What would have happened if, like the *Stella* she had gone down within 10 minutes? People were glad to be back on the shore and even to this day, some of the passengers who had been on the *St Malo* do not like having to go on boats as they find themselves getting nervous and worried.

At one point, the operation seemed in chaos because of the difficulties with communication, Roy Bullen found it hard to co-ordinate the rescue. He tried to find out how many had been taken off the ship and stated that he thought that it was miraculous that nobody had been killed. It was determined that the cause of the crash was human error, because the captain of the *St Malo* took the quickest route. But it was not just human error: Another reason was that there was poor communication from the bridge and that the navigation system was faulty. Also the rocks at high tide could not be seen. Then there was the fact that the vessel was going too fast. It felt to me as if they were passing the buck as no-one wanted to hold their hand up and take responsibility.

The incident could have been seen as a misjudgment on the part of the captain rather than incompetence, but it was a mistake that caused hundreds of people to fear that they would drown. By simple mistakes you can jeopardise so many lives. Of course, a captain's passengers are always going to complain that they wish they'd got home quicker if the sailing is running late, but doesn't that just go with the job's territory? After all, if an accident like this happened again, some of them might not be going home at all.

The 'St Malo' fills with water and begins listing to port

Passengers 'jump' into the life-rafts from a great height causing many injuries

Chapter Three

King Kong or Gentle Giant?

This is a story that captured the hearts of everyone who heard it, not just in Jersey but throughout the United Kingdom and around the world. It is the story of Jambo, a silverback gorilla who in 1986 rose to stardom when a young boy fell into his enclosure at Jersey Zoo (now known as the Gerald Durrell Preservation Trust). What happened next erased any pre-conceived ideas of a gorilla that we might have had, acquired through watching films like Congo, and the unforgettable 1933 version of King Kong, where we witnessed the gigantic pre-historic gorilla unleash a trail of destruction.

Jambo (pronounced 'Yambo') was born on 17th April 1961 in Basel Zoo in Switzerland. His name comes from the Swahili word for 'hello.' Since the day of his birth, Jambo led a remarkable life. He was the first ever Lowland gorilla to be born in captivity in Europe, and to be raised by his birth mother, who was also in captivity but had been born in the wild. It wasn't until 27th April 1972 that Jersey became acquainted with the gorilla, with the help of Gerald Durrell.

Lowland gorillas are the world's largest and most powerful man-like ape. Their natural habitats are tropical rainforests near the equator in Africa. They have a basic healthy diet that consists of berries, leaves and other plants. As they are vegetarians they do not need to eat meat, but have been mistaken for carnivores due to their ferocious faces and sharp teeth. Lowland gorillas are huge: they can weigh up to 200 kilos. It is easy to spot similarities between man and ape, but we are made for different purposes. Gorillas live in the trees and so have a strong bone structure that will support their body weight, whereas humans are constructed to live on the ground, and their skeletons have adapted to 'bipedal locomotion' (standing on two legs.)

Around the world, gorillas' homes are being destroyed by man for timber, farmland and even for property development. It is worrying to think that 21 square kilometres of Africa's forests - the size of a town - are destroyed and wiped out every week. Gorillas are often shot when they trespass onto a farmer's land, but in fact they may have strayed there simply because they are dying of starvation. Even more disturbing is that some countries in the world still have gorilla steak on the menu, and body parts are sold as souvenirs. In 1998 there were less than 1,300 wild gorillas left in the world. Gerald Durrell had always fought for the survival of animals and if it hadn't been for Gerald we would never have met dear old Jambo.

Jambo had a great life at Jersey's Zoo. His keeper, Richard Johnson Scott, looked after him and made sure the gorillas had a healthy, nutritional diet. He fed them fruit and vegetables three times a day, but would also 'forage feed' them in between meals to keep them active and occupied, and to maintain the sort of behaviour they would exhibit in the wild. As a youngster, Jambo was quite small but as an adult he ate at least 27 kilos of food a day. He fathered 15 offspring, 14 of which were born in Jersey. Jambo's first, a male named Tam Tam, had been born to Goma (his female friend) on 2nd May 1971 in Switzerland and it wasn't until two years later that his first baby was born in Jersey. He was called Assumbo and was born to

Nandi on 15th July 1973. Gorillas do not believe in monogamy, and Jambo was a bit of a ladies' man, so it was no surprise that in October that same year a female gorilla named N'pongo gave birth to Mamfe, half-brother to Assumbo. Both infants had to be hand-reared. Gorillas are seen to be devoted parents, and most only have one youngster at a time. Usually one or both of the parents will take care of it until it is old enough to look after itself. Like a human newborn, baby gorillas are helpless and rely on their mothers for nutrition, warmth and protection. A baby gorilla will only weigh about 4 pounds (1.8 kilos). Its skin is pink to begin with, but soon darkens after a few days as its fur begins to thicken. Jambo had three different females to whom he grew emotionally attached - Nandi, N'pongo and Kishka - and this helped a lot with the breeding programme.

On 31st August 1986, Jambo leapt to fame when a young boy named Levan Meritt fell into the gorilla enclosure at Jersey zoo. Levan was on a family holiday with his mother Pauline, father Steve, brother Lloyd and sister Stephanie. The whole world was able to witness this horrifying accident on television and in the newspapers because it was filmed by keen amateur photographer Brian Le Lion. The walls around the enclosure to protect the crowds were chest-high, but little Levan was not tall enough to see. His father lifted him up onto the wall, then turned to his brother to pick him up too. As Levan stood he toppled forward, and plunged off the 20-feet high wall onto a concrete drainage ledge, where he lay unconscious. In shock, Steve attempted to climb down to rescue him but was prevented by other zoo visitors. Blood was coming from the back of Levan's head, and it looked as if he was dead.

As the screams of panic were heard right the way around the zoo, a crowd began to form, many terrified that Jambo would think Levan was an 'enemy' and would attack him. As Jambo drew near, the screams grew louder and people began to pick up rocks and gravel to throw, to try to keep the gorillas at bay. A keeper took control, calmed everyone down, and explained that throwing things would only enrage the animals. Amid the chorus of cries, Jambo carefully descended the grassy slope and approached the small unconscious boy. He stopped on the concrete surround and leant down. He could have literally pulled little Levan apart limb by limb, but instead Jambo carefully sniffed around to see if he or his family were in danger. Once he realised he was safe, he began to gently stroke Levan's still body. The other gorillas gathered around until Rafiki, a youngster, got too close for Jambo's liking. Jambo, who weighed nearly 200 kilos, stood in Rafiki's path to make sure he did not harm this stranger. (Once, when Jambo was unconscious, it had taken seven men to shift him just a few feet, so the message for Rafiki was clear). Jambo sat on his haunches and looked up at the crowd, seeing where this young boy had come from, but not understanding why. Watching everyone scream and shout at him, Jambo calmly looked back at Levan and in true gorilla style began pulling at his clothes and then raised his fingers to his nose to smell them. Levan started to gain consciousness. As he began to cry, he startled the gorillas as well as the spectators. Then he panicked. Jambo, who had been calm throughout this ordeal, now became visibly disturbed. He rose to all fours and paused before moving himself and his family away from the boy. Even the inquisitive Rafiki retreated to the gorilla house.

At the departure of Jambo and his family, the crowd gave a sigh of relief. But that was just the first obstacle out of the way. To everyone's horror Hobbit, the other male silverback, who had been in his quarters, pushed past the females who were trying to get in. This situation needed quick thinking, as Hobbit was known for his mischievous and boisterous behaviour. Showing great courage, keeper Andy Wood took it upon himself to enter the enclosure and position himself next to the boy. He was joined by bird-keeper Gary Clarke. With great teamwork the two men faced down a series of galloping charges from the zoo's second-ranking male gorilla, while ambulance man Brian Fox climbed down to assess Levan's injuries. Brian then signaled, when he was ready, to be hoisted back up to safety by a rope. Rapidly securing the rope around himself he cradled his petrified patient in his arms and was pulled from the enclosure. Both man and boy had successfully escaped, to a roar of applause. Gary and Andy also made a swift exit. Because of the gentleness that Jambo had shown towards his intruder, the story hit international headlines. He became so well known that he was receiving fan mail and even boxes of bananas and various other gifts were delivered to the zoo.

Jambo died on 16 September 1992. The zoo lost a great friend that day, but his memory lives on in recognition of his heroic nature. A statue at the zoo commemorates this wonderful animal. Jambo helped make the zoo a successful breeding-ground for gorillas and Jambo himself was one of the most successful male gorillas in the world to produce so many healthy children. Many of his offspring were sent to other zoos and conservation trusts around the world, to help with the breeding and survival of the species.

Gerald Durrell, who was the founder of Jersey Zoo, believed that smaller and even ugly animals and creatures were in need of protecting against extinction. He found that most commercial zoos tended to have only animals that would please the crowds, such as giraffes and elephants. He was a prolific writer and published various books to help spread the word and works of the Jersey Preservation Trust. Many famous people, including the Princess Royal, have visited the zoo and have been seen enjoying the company of the young gorillas which used to play in Gerald Durrell's garden. When Jambo had his first set of children, they had to be hand-reared as both mothers were born in the wild but raised in captivity. With help from the keepers and from Durrell, the mothers were supported and their babies well-fed. Durrell even let them live in his house, just as if they were his own children, and they were really happy there. Once they grew too big, it was unfair on them to carry on living in the house, and that's when he decided to make an enormous enclosure that would reflect the natural habitat and lifestyle of the animals.

With the help of Jambo's fame, a team of dedicated staff, and Gerald Durrell's patronage, the Trust is able to rescue animals of all shapes and sizes and protect them from extinction. Even though Gerald Durrell has now passed away, the significance and value of his work will live on forever.

Jambo stands guard over Levan and gently strokes him

GORILLA PIT RESCUE EARNS

I was terrified

Hero Brian yesterday

By BARRY GARDNER

BRAVE Brian Fox, who rescued a boy from a gorilla compound, admitted yesterday: " I never thought I would get out alive."

The 34-year-old ambulanceman added: " It was the most terrifying time of my life.

" But thank God we both got out of there all right."

Brian's action was widely praised yesterday and he is to receive a Gold Star Award to mark his courage.

The 15-stone hero jumped 20ft. into the gorilla pit to save five-year-old Levan Merritt.

The boy had fallen over 15ft and lay injured and unconscious among the giant beasts.

Incredibly, they gathered round him and their leader Jambo gently stroked his body.

Brian sprinted 100 yards to the pit after receiving an emergency call at the Jersey zoo.

He said: "By the time I got there, people were shouting and screaming and the boy was unconscious. It was about half a mile to the enclosure gates.

Charging

" I looked over and saw the boy was starting to turn on his back. Once he had done that, he could have choked.

" I could not wait any longer. I just had to jump over the wall. I didn't think about the gorillas. All I could hear was my t... splitting as I went ove...

" I went to check i... All the time this gorill... charging towards ... stopping just a few ... away.

" Two keepers wooden staves were ... to keep him at bay ... they had already se... me if he wanted to c... he would go str... through them and get...

" I was petrified. ... was this hell of a cre... charging around and ... doing my best to sav... boy.

" I was in the pit abo... minutes but it seeme... eternity. I serio... believed I would not g... alive. I positioned mys... cover the boy if the a... attacked us.

"There was talk of g...

STAR

THE FACTS NOT THE FICTION • THURSDAY, SEPTEMBER 4, 1986 **18p** (19p Cls)

...stated. The Star Says—Page 8

KONG BOY'S FEAR

LITTLE Levan Merritt wakes up screaming following his King Kong ordeal after falling into the gorilla pit at Jersey Zoo, his mum Pauline said yesterday.

"It's as if a gorilla is the first thing he sees when he wakes," Mrs Merritt, 29, from Horsham, Sussex, added after visiting her five-year-old son in Southampton hospital.

Gorilla Jambo stroked him as he lay injured in the pit on Sunday.

Levan ... screams

46

ART OF A NATION

Jambo's no Rambo !

He's a big softie
ays his keeper

By BILL GREIG

THE boy who fell into a gorilla pit recovered
om his injuries yesterday, a zookeeper talked
oudly about Jambo the Gentle.

The huge, 25-stone giant gorilla had kept watch over
nnscious five-year-old Levan Merritt after the boy
nged 20ft into the pit at Jersey Zoo. Visitors and TV
wers were astonished to see Jambo gently stroke the
ld and then keep the other shrapes away.

His keeper, Richard Johnson-Scott, said: " He reacted
just the way I would expect him to. We have noticed
ore that the gorillas love children.

" They always react more
favourably to them than
adults. And Jambo is the
most gentle gorilla I have
ever worked with."

And the protective in-
stincts of Jambo—moving
that he's no Rambo among
thrapes—did not surprise
London Zoo's head ape
keeper Mick Carman.

He will only attack to
defend his family."

Safety

And TV naturalist David
Attenborough added :
" After all, a small child is
very much the shape of a
baby gorilla. If it is lying
there motionless, I would
predict the gorilla would
behave in the way he did."

Last night Levan was
stable after surgery for
head injuries at Southampton General Hospital. He
was hauled to safety by
ambulanceman Brian Fox.

Levan's father, Stephen,
from Horsham, Sussex, is
on holiday with his three
other children.

He said yesterday : " I put
Levan on the wall and
turned to pick up one of the
others. He fell and when I
looked down I thought he
was dead."

Picture: TERRY LEDROCK
The Good Guy—Page 8

Levan: 'Stable'

47

Chapter Four

A Meeting with Saddam

Born in Guernsey in 1926, Richard Weithley moved to Jersey when he was just a young boy. He has lived on the Island for most of his life and considers himself a Jersey boy at heart. His career as a quantity surveyor has enabled him to travel the world and he has worked on projects in Egypt, Bulgaria and Kuwait. It was on Saturday 1st August 1990 that Richard arrived in Kuwait with a contract to work on a palace. A busy schedule lay ahead of him. After a good night's sleep at the Maccilla Beach Hotel he made his way down to breakfast, not knowing that Iraqi troops had invaded the country. The first sign that anything was amiss was the arrival of plain-clothed guards carrying pistols and forbidding staff and visitors to leave the hotel. This 'house-arrest' continued for the next couple of days, and it wasn't until the Thursday that troops rounded up everyone and put them on a bus to Basra at 7 o'clock in the morning. Now fully aware of their situation, some people were terrified and others just curious. Around 30 French, Italian and British people were taken from the hotel, among them men, women and children.

When I met Richard he came across as very calm and collected, a good storyteller who does not glamorize his feelings according to what he believes we want to hear. In our discussion, he told me that when they arrived in Basra they had to wait nearly 12 hours until they were put on a train to Baghdad. At this point they were not told why they had been captured, but the troops treated them well and were generous in handing round the beers. Like anyone who has had a little too much to drink, Richard found himself falling asleep. He slept throughout the entire eight-hour train journey, waking to find himself in Baghdad, where they were all sent to a hotel. On Wednesday 15th August the guards got the order to move all the 'prisoners' to workers' accommodation about 30 kilometres from Baghdad. Here the walls and floors were very dirty, and were not very nice to have to live in. Never knowing when they were going to be moved again, it didn't seem too much of a shock when on 18th August they were once again on the move, this time to the office block of a factory that made ammunition outside Baghdad. They were human shields.

One day, when the guards had been running around like headless chickens all morning, they heard a commotion outside. A cardboard cut-out of Saddam Hussein's daughter had been erected in the grounds. At this moment Richard realised what was going on, and knew they were getting a visit from a special guest - but not one you would probably invite to a dinner party. It was Saddam Hussein himself. Richard felt that the cardboard cut-out was there to show his softer side and to show that Saddam liked children. What you expect to hear from most people telling a story about an encounter with Saddam is that they were terrified, but as I have said before, Richard is a man who says what actually happened. In a good-humoured manner, he told me how he found Saddam to be a very charismatic man and could understand why people would see him as a great dictator. However there was still a slight nervous tension, as he also understood how Saddam could have them shot at any time.

Saddam explained the reasoning behind their capture, which was that they were being used as a human shield against the 'vicious enemy' - the British and American troops. Richard felt that Saddam was cheating through his interpreter. He would talk in Arabic, wait for the interpreter to convey this in English, for the prisoners to reply, and then for the reply to be translated back to Arabic: the delay bought him the time he needed to come up with a good answer. On this visit Saddam let all the women and children leave, but all the men had to stay. It was hard for some people, as they were there as part of a family unit. Many women and children were taken from their husbands and fathers, and one woman even tried to get them to let her stay with her husband, but she was not allowed. I felt a sense of confusion when Richard told me this story of his encounter with Saddam Hussein as his comments about the man were unexpected. Was I really hearing someone talk about Saddam and not saying he was all bad?

Once again on 30th August everyone was moved, this time to a large group of villas where more guards and families were already living. This was better accommodation. The prisoners took two of the villas. Richard found himself with three Japanese, two Frenchmen, one American and two British - some were new arrivals. It was at this point that Richard, in order to occupy himself, began to write a children's book, calling it 'The Gobblaters Come to Cliff Top Wood'. Stability didn't last long, as again they were moved into another office block where they remained for the duration of their capture. The thought of being bombed by the Allies was ever present. Richard learned that you had to have your wits about you when it came to the guards, but soon realised that the guards were not able to shoot anyone or harm them, as they would need permission to do so from Saddam. In fact if they had harmed a prisoner they would have been shot themselves.

As the Iraq situation became more hostile, the prisoners embarked on mini-revolutions and many, including Richard, began to break windows, and knock down the posts which supported the barbed-wire fences. One man punched his hand through a door and in doing so, bent his fingers right back. Immediately the people were knocked back in by the rifle-toting guards. Their rations were cut as a punishment. More barbed wire fences were put in place and bars were now welded to every window. Richard is not a big fan of meat, but all they had to eat was meat on skewers. The food had come from far away and so by the time it arrived on the plates, there was mainly only the fat left. Richard lived on coarse bread and dates. The dates were large and very crispy, not like the ones you buy from our supermarkets. Tea and sugar was plentiful but, by this time, Richard was suffering from dizzy spells and had lost nearly 60 pounds.

A dog, which had followed Richard from a previous camp, had given birth to a litter of beautiful puppies but was starving to death. Despite his own desperate need for food, every time Richard had a meal he made sure that he gave the meaty bits to the dogs to ensure their survival. The mother had made a place for her and her puppies underneath Richard's window. As food began to get scarce Richard asked others if they could give him some of theirs so he could feed the dogs. Many said no. The Japanese had food parcels so, feeling a little like a naughty schoolboy, Richard took a little bit of their food so he could feed the dog. As morale dipped further, people started to despair and were stumbling as they walked. To raise their spirits Richard encouraged many of them to play cards together: only simple children's games like 'chase the queen' and 'snap'. The guards let them do this as they were allowed to get up and wander around. The pressure of the constant danger was simply to much for some to bear as one Japanese man was so low that his friends came to Richard to ask for help. Apparently he was lying on his bed facing the wall and was trying to will himself to die. Richard encouraged him to play cards and drink lots of tea, until eventually he began to laugh and smile again. Others also began to break down. Some had been working in Kuwait at the time of their capture and had no more wages to send home and were worried about how their families were coping. Richard was concerned for his wife Marigold, back in Jersey, and his two children.

At times Richard was allowed to play with a football which he kicked about trying to hit different stones. He said he actually became quite good at it by the end. The guards used to play with the football until Richard came outside and they would say 'here you go Mr. Richard, here's your ball.' It's amazing how they could be so polite in that situation. At another point, the battery in his watch had died so he cleverly made himself a sundial. As the days went by, the position of the sun would change. When they were allowed to exercise outside, Richard took with him a handful of stones that he would place near the sundial every time he walked around the building, so he knew how many times he had made the circuit. The guards were bewildered and asked Richard what on earth he was doing. 'I'm measuring up for my escape plan,' he said . They were not impressed and he was shut away for a couple of days. When he came out, he saw that they had demolished the sundial. Occasionally the guards would have a radio so the prisoners could hear music. Then once a week they would watch a film at 4 o'clock on Iraqi television. Richard saw it as their treat for the week. During the latter period of his capture, in November, they were able to phone home once a week. Richard would contact his wife Marigold. Funnily enough, a topic of one of their conversations was about how Richard was worried that he had not been paying into his thrift club, and asked Marigold if she would keep up his payments.

Towards the end of their capture and up to their release, Richard was feeling very ill because he had not been eating. He was taken to hospital for a check-up and was struck by the way the women doctors were very apologetic towards him because they sympathised with his situation. During the period of captivity, one of the British men aged between 60 and 65 died of a heart attack. I asked Richard if, throughout his time as a hostage, he knew what was going on outside and was aware of the war developing. He said that on many occasions he heard the troops practising with their rifles, and even the odd time he would see the search lights scanning the sky, but that was all he knew of outside events. Asking him if he ever tried to escape he said that he knew they were sitting on a pile of bombs:and although he had discovered that he could break off the window bars and flee to the trees if they were ever attacked, there was simply nowhere to go.

The day came that everyone had been hoping for, and on Monday 10th December 1990 they were released. They ended their journey the same way it started, and got the bus back to Baghdad, where they spent a night in a hotel. Eventually Iraq Airlines flew them back to Gatwick. There was a warm welcome for the British men who had been captured. Marigold - and a film crew - met Richard at the airport. There was a reception held for the released prisoners, but Richard didn't attend. If it had been me, I know I would just have wanted to get a good meal and then go straight to bed. He spent one more night in a hotel, the next morning he arrived back safely in Jersey to receive another warm welcome by other relatives and the Bailiff. Overall Richard's ordeal had lasted four and half months. He feels that he has not changed through his experience. 'All experiences are good for you,' says Richard. The fanfare following his release made him into a 'nine-day wonder'. He had lunch at Government House, and everyone wanted him to give a speech. Because Richard is a man who does not take himself too seriously, many people began to get annoyed as they had expected him to be a 'victim', breaking down all the time. How would this have been survival? ITV made a programme of his story called 'Return from Baghdad.'

Richard Weithley is a genuine hero. His laid-back stance on the world enabled him to survive and not break down. This had in fact been his second such like situation as in the Occupation during World War II he had been taken prisoner by the Germans as well. He is an excellent author who has had various books published including a series of children's books 'The Globblaters of Cliff Top Wood' (the book he started to write while in captivity), and the amazing story of his life during the German Occupation called 'So it Was.' By choosing not to let regret dominate his life, but to be a strong-willed survivor, he is an inspiration to many, especially with his philosophy of 'what will be will be.'

Jersey Evening Post

30,219   Vol 101/48   Friday, 24 August, 1990   Price: 26p

Left, Mr Weithley's name and home are announced; centre, the president with the hostages; right, close-up of Mr Weithley

ISLANDER IN IRAQ 'HOSTAGE PARADE'

Quantity surveyor pictured with Saddam Hussein

Saddam Hussein far left, Richard far right with some other hostages

rt of Richard's "nine day wonder" lunch at Government House.
ft to right: Vice Admiral Sir Geofrey Dalton, Richard, The Lieutenant Governor Sir
n Sutton, Ian Cannell, Alan Wicker

Chapter Five

Hitting the Headlines

These are not huge stories; they are not life-changing, nor did they have a huge impact on the Islands. When you read them, you may feel they are some of those tales that you're glad you know about, so that later on you can laugh - or cry - about them over the dinner table with friends. They did however make a bit of a splash in the papers and magazines and were even covered by the ITN, BBC and Sky News teams.

Jumping Mad and Tired Little Ponies

This story was also included in a Channel 4 documentary called " Sports' Dirtiest Secrets" It is a story where luckily no one got hurt, though it still hit the international headlines, perhaps because there were children involved, or perhaps just for the pure stupid nature of what happened. There may even be a moral value in telling this story, because it's a good idea to let others know what people can be like with a competitive head on them. We all have a certain in-built competitive streak and, as children, we naturally develop rivalries. But, let's face it, we're supposed to grow out of it when we're adults. Yes it's fun when watching football, but the people who give the sport a bad name are the ones who turn into football hooligans. And what about show-jumping hooligans? No, surely not - horse-riding is nothing more than a pleasurable hobby.....or is it?

To begin the story, it was a nice Saturday in September 2006. About to take part in the final of the 'under-16 show jumper of the year' competition were nearly 30 children and their horses. The event was held by the British Show Jumping Association (BSJA) who were in charge of the junior championships qualifying round. Everything seemed normal as the kids were dressing and preparing their horses ready to start. It wasn't until one parent allegedly saw something fall from her horse's mouth that suspicions began to be aroused. Worried about safety, the woman looked closer and picked up what looked to her like a horse sedative. Now everyone was concerned. Allegations started flying and someone reported seeing one of the mothers handing out what they assumed were mints to all the horses. People remarked on how lethargic some of the horses were and how they had been behaving oddly. The competition was immediately suspended.

The BSJA inspector, Richard Bree, carried out an investigation to see if the allegations were true. He employed the help of chief vet Tim Hubbard, who took blood samples from each horse. It came as a shock when they discovered that the animals had in fact been drugged with acetylpromazine, a drug used to calm nervous horses. What was thought to be an important, but basically friendly, event had now turned into a vicious, stop-at-nothing competition. The chief vet advised all the parents and children not to ride their horses for at least 36 hours until they would be guaranteed to be clear of the drug. As the animals were led back into their trailers, an onlooker reported seeing one horse so disorientated that it needed assistance.This shows just how serious it could have been if the contest had gone ahead.

The BSJA took the matter very seriously and said that if they could prove an offence had been committed that brought the sport into disrepute, the guilty party would be fined and possibly even suspended. It may seem harsh that it would be the child who would suffer, who after all had nothing to do with his mother's bizarre actions: the parent brought this upon her child and should take full responsibility. In the end she escaped punishment because the police decided they could not take any further action as there is no law against 'horse-doping'. My question would be, is this fair? This parent put nearly 30 children in peril, because a doped horse might have fallen on them when jumping. The horses were in danger too - we all know what happens to horses with broken legs. It has been reported that a number of parents are considering suing in a civil action.

If rivalries begin to occur in these competitive children's sports, what kind of future do they have? After jeopardising the good name of show-jumping in the Island, would it really be such a surprise if the organisers decided to cancel the event for good? You will be glad to know that they did in fact reschedule the competition and the children were able to take part. When this story first hit the papers, the usual rumours began circulating: one I heard was that the mother who had done this really needn't have bothered, because her child needed no extra help as he was tipped to win anyway. Isn't it funny how some people's minds work? If all this proves to be true I think a check-up from the neck up is called for!

Lost and Found Out

This story is a far cry from the typical tale of misfortune at sea: in fact it could rival the script for the movie 'Open Water', but with a bizarre twist

What does it take to fake your own disappearance? A great deal of knowledge and preparation, time and effort? The particular disappearance I'll tell you about bore none of these hallmarks - just a great deal of stupidity and lies. First of all, I'll set out the story of what happened to the missing diver off Guernsey, and then I'll bring you back to reality by revealing the truth.

It began with a 35-year-old man who was reported missing on Saturday 2nd September 2006 after he failed to arrive home from a day's diving. His wife was extremely worried, as Matthew had gone diving by himself, so her main fear was that he was in danger. A major sea and air rescue operation was launched. As time passed, the hopes of finding Matthew alive faded as the water temperature was only 17 degrees centigrade.

Apparently that morning Matthew re-surfaced from a dive at Fermain Bay when he was hit by a boat, which sped off and left him unconscious in the water. He was swept out by the tide miles from the coast, then later got caught on some rocks east of Petit Port. Throughout the next three days he was stranded there, lapsing in and out of consciousness.

On Monday morning, Matthew decided he had to do something if he was going to survive, as he was too exhausted to climb the rocks he decided to let the tide carry him again, hopefully this time back towards Fermain. He was then spotted by a yacht around 7pm that day. Steve and Anne-Marie Westwood had been watching a pod of dolphins off Fermain when they noticed something floating in the water, and sped to the rescue.When questioned about his equipment, Matthew said he had lost his mask together with the regulator which controls the air supply. He had ditched his weight-belt and tank in his attempt to swim out of the current which had been pulling him away from the coast. After being treated for exhaustion at Princess Elizabeth Hospital, Matthew was able to delight his family and the press with the 'story' of his amazing ordeal.

As he had escaped injury, the police saw no reason to investigate the incident any further. In the delight (and the newspaper headlines) that greeted the news of his survival, a few thought that there might be something fishy going on. Guernsey harbour-master Captain Peter Gill, for example was astonished by Matthew's story: he said he had never heard of anyone being pulled from the sea alive after 58 hours.

I don't want to sound as if I'm fighting for justice and all that palava, but here's what really happened. Matthew had lied to his wife about his scuba-diving plans. She had not been suspicious because he was an experienced diver who was used to diving alone. (I'm not a professional diver but even I know that there is a huge health and safety issue in there somewhere). On that Saturday morning Matthew had taken a ferry over to Poole on the UK mainland, returning on the Monday morning and putting himself into the waters off Guernsey where he allowed himself to be 'rescued.' by the passing yacht. He was found out because a member of the public had spotted him in Dorset and recognised him from the pictures of the 'missing diver' She called the police. He was also seen at a self-storage facility in Poole: the staff of Lok'n'Store told police that Matthew had dropped off some scuba-diving equipment into a storage holder that weekend.

When questioned again by the police, he admitted the elaborate hoax. Rumours began to circulate, as they do in a small community: was Matthew involved in an affair, or drug-smuggling. Was he the perpetrator of a big robbery in the UK? The police found no evidence of foul play and later stated that no charges would be brought against him. Captain Peter Gill, who was the search co-ordinator, said he was pleased that no-one was hurt, but was nevertheless angry about the hoax.

Certainly his friends and family suffered. They had been told it would be a miracle if Matthew turned up alive after 58 hours in the water. So for nearly three days they believed he was dead. When he was found, there was a news story showing Matthew's father, in floods of tears thanking the yachtsmen who found him. If Matthew is not well then my sincere sympathy goes out to him and his family, and I hope for his good health.

If it was just a stupid act, we have to remember the people who risked their lives to save this man and who put their reputations on the line. The lifeboat operators were criticised, as the public claimed that they did not do their job properly. High-tech tidal flow charts were used to try to locate him but to no avail. Over those few days, several hundred people were out looking for Matthew: the Channel Island Air Search, the *Flying Christine* Lifeboat, the general public and even police divers.

If this hoax had been perpetrated by a young person, it would not have been met with such tolerance and he would have suffered a huge punishment for his act of stupidity. Yet this was an adult - and aren't adults supposed to know better? I know you can't put a price on someone's life, but his three-day 'adventure' cost the rescue services £10,000. Surely he should have faced a community service order to help others, if not a hefty fine? But this is just my opinion and I'm sure you will have your own.

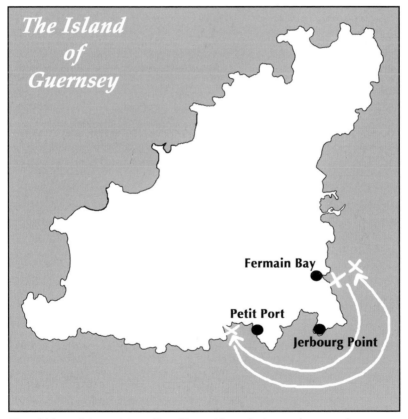

He said in a statement to police: "I must have lost consciousness because the next thing I remember I was quite some distance offshore and caught in the tide running south/southwest past Jerbourg"

The Man Who Fell To Earth

What an amazing thing survival is. To slip out of death's hands and live to tell the tale. It is always extraordinary when we hear about people surviving earthquakes or tidal waves (hardly a feature of Jersey's climate!) but some stories really make you believe in miracles. This is one of them: it's about a young guy who defeated death from 15,000 feet - that's a two-mile fall. I am not a big fan of heights, or jumping out of planes, but this story is one in a million. So don't try this at home.

Twenty-five-year-old Michael Holmes had jumped out of many planes before. Whenever an opportunity arose he'd jump. The Jerseyman, who has emigrated to New Zealand, simply lives for skydiving. He is a professional and the youngest British person ever to qualify as a skydiving instructor. Like all professionals, he believes in a good health and safety check before any dive.

On the 12th December 2006 Michael, his best friend John King, and a plane full of students, took to the skies. It was to be a routine jump where, at 15,000 feet, they would exit the plane and freefall for about one minute. The parachute cord would then be pulled at 4,000 feet - sufficient height to correct anything should there be a problem. Michael was the first to jump, closely followed by John. Both had cameras in their helmets to capture the excitement. What was in the camera by the time they reached the ground, however, was not exactly the footage they had anticipated.

A skydiver's parachute is connected to a container on his back by multiple lines: pulling on the cord causes the container to spring open and the parachute to burst out. When Michael Holmes pulled the cord, nothing happened. He quickly realised that the lines had got tangled and this had caused the container to stick. Not too stressed, as it had happened on a couple of occasions before, he did the usual drill and pulled on the reserve cord when he was 1,000 feet above the ground. He deployed the reserve but the reserve couldn't deploy itself either because of the tangle. There was no more backup to call on - he was hurtling straight for the ground, and being thrown through the air like a rag-doll.

The video footage of Michael shows his body spinning round and round, and the ground getting closer by the second. He had fallen from 15,000 feet at 120mph. At that moment, as he saw his shadow on the ground getting bigger and bigger, Michael was certain he was going to die. Unlike many people, he did not see his life flash before his eyes but felt frustrated at the thought that his life was going to end this way. With the very few seconds that he had left, he struggled to find the words he wanted to tell his family and friends, but the camera only records him waving and saying 'bye'. Just 30 seconds after his reserve parachute failed to open, Michael smashed into the ground. He landed in a blackberry bush in a conservation area in Five-Mile Bay in Taupo on New Zealand's North Island.

Through the lens of John King you see a compelling view of the scene he witnessed: a heart-wrenching picture of what he thought were Michael's last few seconds of life. He was not unduly worried when he saw his friend struggle to open the main parachute, but when he realised that he had still not managed to open his reserve just a couple of hundred feet from the ground, he was certain Michael would die. There was nothing John could do, except to steer himself into the same blackberry bush where his friend had crash-landed.

He crawled through eight feet of blackberry bush to try and get to Michael as quickly as he could. When he saw Michael's unconscious body, it was blanketed by the parachute. At this point he believed that Michael was dead or knocking on death's door. He uncovered his friend's body and began to shout at him to see if he could get any reaction. To his astonishment, Michael came round almost instantly. John tried to reassure him and keep him awake until the ambulance arrived. The fire brigade was also called, as they needed to slash a path through the brambles so the ambulance crew could get Michael out safely.

It is miraculous that Michael survived the horrific fall, but what was more amazing was his injuries - or, rather, the lack of them. You can imagine the devastation that falling from 15,000 feet at 120mph could cause to the body. At the hospital Michael was treated only for a broken ankle and a collapsed right lung: serious injuries, but not life-threatening.

John King feels that his friend was a 'very lucky boy', particularly because he came down in that exact spot. If he had landed just a few feet to either side of the blackberry bushes, it would have been a very different story. On one side was ocean, which would have been like hitting concrete: if the impact had not killed him, then he would have drowned. Talking about concrete, on the other side was a car park where he wouldn't have stood a chance. Even so, there was an enormous amount of luck in falling on that particular spot, as there were tree stumps dotted all around the bramble bush - one was found close to his head. The size of the bramble bush cushioned his fall slightly but, even then, if he had fallen awkwardly he could have broken his back or even his neck. He had been at the complete mercy of gravity. This was a million to one shot and he lived to tell the story. Michael, too, considers himself to be very lucky and finds it rather surreal that he survived. Even after such an horrific experience, once Michael was fit and healthy he wanted to get straight back on a plane and jump again. After more than 7,000 jumps, he did not feel the need to stop over 'one little hitch'. When reflecting on the camera footage of his fall Michael said, "It's awesome, in a sadistic kind of way. I suppose you have to laugh about it and not dwell for the rest of your life on what might have happened". The family have their worries and concerns, but say that they would be more worried if Michael didn't go back to the sport he loves.

This incredible photo is from Michael's helmet camera and shows the ground rushing towards him at over 120mph. He thought his last act would be to wave goodbye to his family

Chapter Six

As Time Goes By
by guest writer Jeff Le Caudey

Some of the following tales were real headline-grabbers in their day, but by and large they were soon forgotten. They do however have two things in common: they were tragic for the people involved and many were rather unusual - even curious.

At Sea

Over the centuries there have been hundreds of shipwrecks and countless unfortunates have drowned in Channel Island waters. You will read about some of them elsewhere in this book. Here, I would like to tell you of some of the more curious of those tales.

In 1850, the steam tug *Polka* was on her way to St Malo when she was discovered to be leaking. The crew quickly altered course and headed for the Les Minquiers, a group of rocks situated between Jersey and France, which were home to a few fishermen's cottages. The 50 passengers were transferred by lifeboat to the islets in the nick of time. Minutes later the tug sank. Quite soon the passengers and crew were rescued and taken on to France - so far, so good.

The tug's captain had only agreed to pilot the leaky vessel as a means of getting to France, where he was due to pick up

The Superb, which had been undergoing repairs. When *The Superb* duly set sail for Jersey, the passengers - who had heard the story of the wreck -persuaded the captain to show them where it had happened. It was a fatal mistake. Just off Les Minquiers, the ship hit submerged rocks. In the ensuing panic, some passengers took to the lifeboats and some elected to stay on board. Twenty of those who decided to leave the stricken vessel drowned when two lifeboats overturned. Those who stayed aboard were safe - the ship remained stuck on the rocks, high and fairly dry.

*

More lives were lost on a St Malo run in 1905 when *The Hilda*, a 20-year-old iron steamship, struck rocks in a blizzard. Some 128 lives were lost, making it a tragedy, of course, but also a fairly regular occurrence in those treacherous waters. What gave a macabre twist to the matter was the way a French firm, deciding to profit from the disaster, produced and sold a set of postcards showing not only the wreck, but the body of the captain.

*

What people described as 'the most terrible drowning tragedy ever' occurred in the afternoon of 7th July 1915 at Jersey's Portelet Bay. Twenty boys from Highlands College chapel choir had left town, accompanied by their music master and bursar, on their way to their annual picnic at Portelet. It was a two-hour journey, and when the party arrived around 4pm, the boys decided to swim or paddle.

Boisterous wind and rough seas did not deter the lads and soon most of them were in the water. Suddenly, cheerful shouts and laughter turned to screams as waves and undertow swept several of the boys off their feet. In seconds they were out of their depth. The two masters, both men of the cloth, dashed into the water along with several men working on the nearby Portelet farm. A boat was launched and a number of boys who were being carried out by the strong current were pulled aboard. One boy, who the bursar had only just managed to drag ashore, saw his younger brother struggling and rushed back into the water to save him. By the time Dr Bentliff arrived from town by car, the survivors had been given artificial respiration, but eight were dead - including the young hero who had attempted to save his brother's life.

*

It was 1938, and a Second World War was looming when a Royal Navy warship anchored out in St Aubin's Bay. Eager to get onto dry land even for a short while, several ratings came ashore in the liberty boat, which they moored in St Helier Harbour. It was dark when the time came to return. As they headed out of the harbour they couldn't actually see their ship, and they may have thought it had been 'blacked out' or had moved its moorings. We will never know, because what they didn't realise was that the Elizabeth Castle breakwater was between them and the warship. At full speed they smashed into the solid stone wall. No-one survived.

*

Many years before the liberty boat tragedy, a man was employed to keep a light burning on the Elizabeth Castle breakwater. He was provided with a lamp, fuel and free accommodation in the castle. But there was a down side to this easy, if boring job - he was not permitted to go ashore once the light had been lit. So why, two nights before Christmas, did he quietly launch his old rowing boat and head for the harbour? Was it thoughts of the fleshpots of St Helier and the warmth of Christmas hospitality at his favourite tavern that seduced him from his duties? Again we will never know - his body was washed up on Jersey's southeast coast and his boat was never found.

*

That the 1,100 ton German ship S.S Schoktland sank a mile south-west of Noirmont point on 5th January 1943 is fact - why remains a mystery. The passengers were mainly German soldiers going on leave during the Occupation. There was no attack by Allied forces. One claim is that it struck rocks while awaiting an escort Considering the speed with which the ship sank it must have been very badly damaged. Of the 336 passengers and crew on board, only 178 survived. Four of these had drifted on a raft onto Les Minquiers and were rescued several days later. One soldier who survived lost all the fingers on his right hand: they had been severed by an iron door, which slammed on him as the ship suddenly listed. 'Sinel's War Diary' says that, after the war, it was claimed that the ship had been deliberately blown up. The perpetrators were said to be workers under the control of Organisation Todt, a semi-military group who commanded a forced-labour team of mainly Spanish political prisoners. Shortly after the sinking, a friend of mine, who acted as interpreter between the various nationalities, told me that someone referred to only as the 'Golden Spaniard,' had placed a hand-grenade under floorboards in the hold near a stack of explosives. He had attached a string to the firing pin and fed the string up through a crack to lie innocently on the deck - until a tidy sailor spotted it and pulled it out. Other German sources say the ship ran into Les Grunes aux Dardes due to bad navigation which is more likely.

*

In 1960 the *Jean Rose*, a newly built 14-foot speed-boat, was undergoing sea-trials in St Aubins Bay. It was a fine day and several friends had taken the opportunity to come along for the ride. Deciding to see what the boat could do, the skipper opened the throttle wide. Normally this would cause the bow to lift, the stern to dip and the boat to take off at a rate of knots - not this time. Unaccountably the boat suddenly nose-dived and turned turtle. Of the seven on board, only one man and a dog survived.

*

A tragedy coupled with a remarkable feat of endurance occurred in 1964. When the *Mariecelia* was struck by hurricane-force winds off the southwest coast of Jersey, the crew of five was swept overboard. The Jersey lifeboat, together with *HMS Curzon*, a Royal Navy vessel on exercise in the area, rushed to the scene, but all they found was the stricken yacht motoring slowly in circles. There was no sign of life. A massive search was organised with helicopters and in-shore rescue craft, but no survivors were found at the scene.

However, no-one realised how the run of tides, winds and current had combined to sweep the crew around the coast. As Alison Mitchell, a young girl, drifted in the water, she saw her companions die, one by one. The shore remained tantalisingly out of reach - she was so close that she could see the traffic lights changing, but she was at the mercy of the sea. After 18 hours, half blinded by salt and with her body swollen by the water, she was carried ashore by the currents at Petit Port on the north coast of Jersey.

Somehow she managed to struggle up the steep path from the beach and found help at a farmhouse. It is estimated that she must have drifted between 15 and 20 miles during her 18-hour ordeal. It was a remarkable survival.

On the Railway

Trains also caused their share of casualties. Around a dozen people lost life or limb by coming into contact with the locomotives of the Jersey railways.

A farmer leading his horses across the track was hit and killed, but the horses escaped injury. The local trains of those days travelled quite slowly compared with the high-speed monsters in the UK, so one wonders how anyone could fail to have seen or heard them coming.

On one occasion a mother living near the track heard frantic whistling from an approaching engine. Glancing out of the kitchen window, she was horrified to see her baby daughter Katie happily sitting on the track playing with a doll. With a turn of speed only to be found in dire emergency, she reached the line and scooped the baby up just as the train rolled by. In a similar situation, another child was not so lucky and lost both legs.

The last to be killed by a train in Jersey was a farmer in 1943. He was crossing one of the network of tracks laid across his fields by the Germans, when he was struck by an engine pushing a line of trucks - he never heard them coming because the poor man was stone deaf.

On the Roads

There was a number of small bus companies on the Islands in the 1920s and 1930s, all competing for business. This led to speeding, risk-taking and overtaking - and sometimes straight to the undertaker.

One notorious bus crash happened at the bottom of Mt.Felard in 1931 when a JMT single-decker went out of control coming down the steep hill. The bus crashed into a wall and overturned near Stanley Benest's Grocery, now Benest's of Millbrook. Police, ambulance and fire brigade personnel were soon on the scene, but they faced a daunting task. Fifteen people had been injured, seven seriously. Two of the women died later in hospital and, at the inquest, a passenger said the driver appeared to be struggling with the gears but the bus got faster and faster. The driver, Mr East, told how the brakes didn't seem to be holding and it kept jumping out of gear. At the bottom of Mt Felard, he tried to turn left in a desperate attempt to avoid someone standing on the pavement opposite. It was then that the bus tipped over onto its side.

A passer-by told how the engine of the wrecked bus was roaring and the gear was in neutral. There seemed to be bodies and blood everywhere and people were screaming. It was quite an old bus which might account for the gears jumping out, and was fitted with only two wheel brakes. In an interesting insight into a bit of social history, it was stated in the Evening Post report that, on hearing the crash, one witness 'ran out of his house without his hat!'

*

A practice drill turned to tragedy at Jersey Airport in 1945 when the fire tender turned over, killing three firemen and injuring two. The timed drill was carried out most days after the last flight had departed. It consisted of driving at speed to a given point on the runway and then coupling up the hose in the shortest possible time. On this Sunday, as the driver turned the tender just short of the objective, it suddenly rolled over. Three of the crew were injured as they were thrown clear, but the other three, including the driver, were crushed beneath the vehicle. They left three widows and nine children. A German doctor and several German soldiers from the nearby POW camp rushed to the scene and helped attend the injured firemen until more help arrived.

*

In 1955, The Bouley Bay Hill Climb claimed the life of Australian Bill Sleeman when his supercharged Mini Cooper hit a bank and turned over. Spectators and officials rushed to right the racing car and free the driver, suspecting that, as in the past, he would emerge shaken and bruised but grinning - this time the driver had not survived.

*

A few years earlier, at Jersey's International Road Race, driver KW Bear died when his Bugatti ran out of road at Bel Royal corner, taking the lives of a police sergeant and a doctor with him. It is thought that his brakes failed as he attempted to slow for that rather tricky bend. Desperately he tried to take evasive action, but his car crashed into the wall where the other two victims were standing.

*

In the mid-1960s an item in the Evening Post announced that the 100th motor accident had occurred at the corner of Janvrin Road and St Mark's Road. Tickners Corner had been hit again - in just about every one of those accidents, one of the vehicles involved had ploughed into Tickners shop doorway!

At War

One would expect tragic stories during war time but the next stories are both macabre and curious.

At 2pm on a busy Saturday, an unlucky man and a very unlucky horse were killed in the heart of St Helier by a cannon ball - but that was in 1643. For some reason (boredom perhaps?) the Royalists who were in possession of Elizabeth Castle had decided to fire a volley or two onto the town. While everyone else dived for cover, this unfortunate man just stood there. A cannon ball killed him outright then ricocheted on and killed a horse as well.

*

The British army has never been noted for its soft or humane approach to defaulters, especially deserters. An incident which took place at Elizabeth Castle a few hundred years ago can really only be described as barbaric. The garrison comprised a mixture of English and Jersey soldiers. After a mortar bomb fired from the Town Hill had destroyed most of the castle's supplies of ammunition and food, several soldiers panicked and tried to desert - five were recaptured.

As a lesson to all it was decided that two of these men would hang. Lots were drawn using slips of paper which were either blank or had a noose drawn on it. One Jerseyman and one Englishman were selected to die. Immediately the other English soldiers rescued their countryman and refused to give him up - the Jersey lad was not so lucky. Again lots were drawn and another Jersey soldier was chosen. Here is the barbaric part: the second lad was ordered to hang his comrade by pushing him off the battlements with a noose round his neck, the other end being attached to a cannon. Had he refused, no doubt he too would have hanged.

*

In the early hours of 9th June 1944, four German soldiers were on guard duty at Seymour Tower on Jersey's east coast. The men were fully equipped with helmets, great coats, boots and weapons. They were prepared to face any enemy. These unfortunate men left it too late leaving their post to return to dry land at the end of their watch. By the time the men realised that the waters had surrounded them they were stuck on rocks, it was too late. Laden as they were, there was no escape.

Their shouts were heard from the shore and local fishermen, experienced in the ways of this treacherous bit of coast, immediately offered to launch a boat and rescue the trapped men. Incredibly their offer was refused by the German authorities who instead launched a boat at Gorey, nearly three miles away, and manned it with inexperienced German soldiers.

On arrival they found nothing. After the tide had receded, the bodies of the four soldiers, still fully equipped, were found at the foot of the rock on which they had been standing. The Oberfeldweble in charge of the party had died almost one month to the day before his 30th birthday.

*

The German horse-drawn cart was ambling at a leisurely pace down Val Plaisant in St Helier. It was 1944 ,the day was cold and the driver sat huddled in his fieldgrey army greatcoat. He was not in a hurry and neither were the two large Belgian horses. A German officer striding up Val Plaisant glanced disparagingly at the rather scruffy looking turnout, then his disapproval turned to anger when the *Schweinhund* of a driver passed him by without saluting. Swivelling on his heel, the officer bellowed 'Halt.' Neither the driver nor the horses paid the slightest attention to him. Furious now, the officer spotted two soldiers further down the road. On his order one took the horse's bridle while the other pulled on the brake. As the rig came to a stop, the driver toppled slowly forward - he was stone dead.

By Their Own Hand

From the beginning of the twentieth century, until the Second World War, 1,200 desperate people in Jersey alone committed or attempted to commit suicide. If you survived, the punishment was four to six weeks' hard labour.

Many hanged themselves, often with their own belt, but the second favourite was drowning. Curiously, for an Island surrounded by water, several attempted it in the bath tub.

In 1911 there were two rather unusual efforts at ending it all. A young man named Priestly, an undergraduate at Oxford who was intending to enter the priesthood, suddenly threw himself onto the railway track in front of the train approaching Don Bridge station. The train missed his head but completely crushed his left foot which was later amputated.

Later that year a Mr Trachy went to the quarry at Westmount and shot himself six times. One bullet lodged in his skull and another in the roof of his mouth. He was found unconscious but when the police arrived, amazingly he was able to walk with them to the police station. He died two days later.

Even More Curious

In this day and age constipation, although a miserable affliction, can usually be sorted by a trip to the chemist for an off-the-shelf remedy. In 1899 however Mr Henry Boyed either did not know a chemist or thought he knew best. Unfortunately, his DIY method proved fatal. He took a bottle of Spirits of Salts, the liquid used to clean out drains, diluted it with water and quaffed the lot, safe in the knowledge that, if it could clear pipes, it would cure his complaint. After a night of extreme agony and despite the attendance of two doctors, the poor man died in the early hours of the morning.

*

Spontaneous human combustion is hardly an everyday occurance, but a young girl saw it with her own eyes early one morning in 1919. The child, who lived at No 6 Rouge Bouillon was in the habit of taking a cup of tea up to an elderly lady lodger who lived alone on the top floor. As usual at 7am she knocked on the door and went in. The sight that met her must have stayed with her for the rest of her life. The entire room had been gutted by fire and the elderly lady's blackened corpse still lay on the burned-out bed. Strangely the fire had not spread outside the room, no-one had heard any unusual sounds, and no-one had smelt smoke.

*

In its day, West Park Pavilion was a well-known venue for concerts, ballroom dances, tea dances, shows and beauty competitions. In 1923 it was the scene of a tragedy. The place was packed with spectators, nearly all men who had come to enjoy the sight of two heavyweight boxers, Cashil Craig and Wally Ralph, battling it out for the Jersey heavyweight boxing challenge. It was a title that Wally held, but the winner would challenge for the Channel Islands heavyweight title.

Although Wally Ralph was obviously the better man, Cashil Craig stood up well. The battle went on for 19 gruelling rounds, then - at the beginning of the 20th - Cashil suddenly collapsed. Had the maximum number of rounds been restricted to 12, as it is today, perhaps this tragedy might have been averted. As it was, Cashil Craig died in hospital. There was a rumour at the time that Cashil had never actually boxed professionally before - he had just entered the challenge for the money!

*

Considering the volume of air traffic to and from the Island, Jersey has been lucky to have had comparatively few accidents. The first fatal accident to occur resulted in the death of nine-year-old Denis Dutot in August 1934. At that time the 'airport' was West Park beach, the departure lounge was an old coach and there was a weighing machine for the luggage. Young Denis was playing happily with a friend near the sea wall when a Jersey Airways DH Rapide, heading along the beach at speed for take-off, suddenly veered off course and crashed into the sea wall. Denis Dutot died instantly and his young friend was seriously injured. The plane itself suffered very little damage.

*

We are all used to seeing dramatic or amusing special effects on TV or at the cinema. The fact that they can go wrong, or even be extremely dangerous, seldom occurs to us. A few of you might still remember that Billy Cotton and his 'Billy Cotton Band show' was filmed in Jersey in 1964, and it was then that a stunt went wrong.

The idea was that a piano should be towed through the country lanes with smoke belching from it. There would then be a minor explosion with more smoke and a bang - but it was not to be! The amount of explosive secreted in the piano was far greater than anyone realised. The explosion sent bits of piano 150 feet in all directions and put six people in casualty at the General Hospital, including a technician and three extras. Billy Cotton was knocked flat on his ample back - the piano never recovered.

*

84

Some stunts are more of a fiasco than a tragedy. The saying 'just a bunch of cowboys' probably had a different meaning in 1924, but when Montana Bob's Rodeo came to Springfield, Jersey, the end-product was about the same. First Montana Bob and two of his 'cowboys' arrived without horses. He blamed the authorities who would not allow the animals to travel to the Island. Then he decided to use whatever local horses were available for hire, which was not the best idea as, in trick-riding, man and horse need to build a rapport. It was rumoured that even a cart-horse was pressed into service! Springfield was packed solid, the Lieutenant Governor arrived and the show began. It was reported later that although one or two of the displays raised some applause, in general it was slow and unexciting. It was noticed, however, that despite the local vet's warnings, spurs had been fitted and one horse had a rope tied tightly around its middle. These devices were used to 'encourage' the poor animal to buck. A saddle girth snapped, the rider went flying, and a totally fed-up riderless horse decided to leave - and it didn't care by what route! As it careered around the arena the animal spotted the way it had come in. Regardless of the people now filling the narrow passageway, the horse went straight for the gap and attempted to take the crowd at a jump. Men, women and children were bowled over and thrown to the ground as the horse attempted to make good its escape.

When the horses were examined they were found to have several cuts caused by spurs. Bob Montana (Joseph Roberts) was arrested and charged with cruelty. He received a heavy fine and was asked not to return.

Tragedies Averted

To be shot by a jealous lover could be described as bad luck - for your life to then be saved by your braces, must be described as a miracle.

The jealous sharp-shooter, Jules Paillardon, was angry because his girlfriend Marie had rejected him - so he waited for her in the cowshed with a gun. When Marie and her boss, Farmer Paul Le Petit, arrived at milking time the man opened fire. Marie was hit twice but managed to run away. The bullet aimed at Mr Le Petit amazingly ricocheted harmlessly off the brass buckle of his braces! Possibly hoping for 'third time lucky' the unhappy Jules Paillardon then shot himself in the head. He died later. Marie survived her injuries.

*

What would you think your life was worth? Many insure themselves for thousands of pounds, yet at the beginning of the last century, a Jersey farmer did not seem to put much value on it.

While driving his cart up Conway Street in St Helier, he fell from his seat and rolled under the hooves of his horses. The two animals, frightened and confused by his sudden appearance beneath their feet, began to rear up and prance about. The man was in dire danger of being trampled to death - but tragedy was averted. Seeing the situation and regardless of the flying hooves, a cabby from the Broad Street rank, rushed forward and dragged the now semi-conscious man clear. As the farmer recovered from his ordeal, the cabby washed and bandaged his cuts and applied ointment to the multiple bruises: a glass of something to steady the nerves was also supplied. Once he was back on his feet, the grateful man rewarded the cabby with one old penny, possibly the equivalent today of 70p. Not a lot for a life, but then farmers have always claimed to be short of money!

*

In 1915, the Great War was at its height. While British and French troops faced the German forces across the desolate mud of no-man's land, a lance corporal dispatch rider lay asleep on a mattress in the District Office at Fort Regent. The District Office was the communication and administration HQ for the military authority in Jersey. Telephones were not widely in use, so the telegraph and motorcycle dispatch riders were the main source of military communication. It was mid morning as the lance corporal dozed on his mattress and two of his colleagues sat at a table playing cards. Suddenly as the door crashed open, there was a yell of 'dispatch rider!'

The sergeant in charge was normally a quiet, reserved man and the note of desperation in his voice was so out of character that the card players stared open-mouthed. The lance corporal was quicker to react - he was on his feet and running. As the sergeant thrust the dispatch into the man's hand he said: 'It's the troopship. It's leaving the Albert Quay now, and the Admiralty reckon there are German submarines waiting outside.'

As the motorcycle tore down Pier Road and across the Weighbridge, the rider could see smoke rising from the ship's funnels. She was ready to sail. When he reached the top of the Albert Pier his heart sank - it looked as if half the Island had turned out to wave goodbye to the departing soldiers. His way was completely blocked by a mass of shouting, cheering humanity - and the ship was beginning to move.

The young lance corporal knew that at all costs he must get the warning to the troopship, but he also knew that tooting his horn would never be heard by the excited well-wishers. Quickly changing down a gear, he opened the throttle wide and charged straight at the crowd. The bellow from the semi-open exhaust of that powerful old machine sounded like a thunderclap. As he roared towards them, the crowd began to part, leaving a narrow passageway; he went through the gap at speed. Skidding to a stop, he dropped his motorcycle to the ground and ran to the edge of the pier. He was just able to push the dispatch into the outstretched hand of a crew member leaning over the rail of the moving ship. Minutes later orders were shouted, the telegraph tinkled, the engines were reversed and the troopship slid slowly back to its berth on the Albert Quay - tragedy had been averted.

A little over a week later, while delivering an urgent message to the States Buildings, the same dispatch rider took a short cut across the Royal Square in St Helier. He was fined half a crown at the Town Hall.

*

A party of 11 visitors were enjoying their afternoon at St Brelade. It was a fine day and the tide was high. There was plenty of laughing and splashing as the swimmers frolicked in the warm waters at the Ouaisne end of the beach - they didn't realise the dangers of the heavy swell and the undertow. Suddenly their enjoyment turned to fear as a sudden surge of water dashed the whole group against the rocks. One man was dragged further by the undertow and carried some distance from shore. Amid the screams and cries for help, another member of the party swam strongly to the struggling man.

It was then that a figure was noticed sprinting towards the scene - Constance Brown, complete with her trusty surf-board was about to make her 11th rescue. When she reached the two swimmers, one of them decided he could make it to shore unaided, so Constance concentrated on supporting the other on her board. Then she saw that the first man was becoming exhausted in his fight against the undertow, she managed to get him onto her board too. Totally spent now and unable to swim back to the beach, Constance, with the aid of her board, supported both men until help arrived. All three were finally pulled back to safety with a lifeline.

On another occasion Miss Brown rescued a family of three from drowning, and only just made it back against the undertow.

She had first taken to the water at a swimming pool in Harrogate, but the experience terrified her. She persevered and eventually learned to swim in her home town of Blackburn - a far cry from Jersey's sometimes wicked seas. From the time she arrived in Jersey in 1926 aged 15, until she hung up her surf-board 32 years later, Constance Brown conducted 30 rescues in St Brelade's Bay. She earned the Humane Society Medal and Bar, the Scout Silver Cross and Bar and the MBE - not bad for someone who used to be afraid of water. This gallant lady died in 1984.

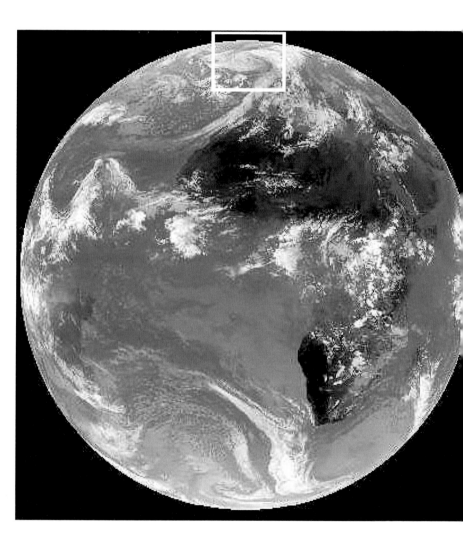

Chapter Seven

The Great Storm

Imagine waking up and seeing a tree crashing through your bedroom window, or watching as the roof of your house is swept off right in front of your very eyes. These experiences were witnessed by many in the Channel Islands during the Great Storm and could have been a scene straight out of 'Twister'. It wreaked mass devastation and affected the whole of the UK. Luckily for me, I was only a baby when it happened in 1987 and have no recollection of it, but it brought tragedy to many families, some of whom found it a struggle to piece their lives together again. If asked, most people will remember the night well and have a story of their own to tell about it. It was the worst storm not just in living memory, but for over 280 years. The last recorded storm of this magnitude was back in 1703.

It was first noticed in the Bay of Biscay off the north coast of Spain. Meteorologists believed it to be a typical depression caused by Africa's warm air meeting the cold air from the North Atlantic, but it was not typical at all. Many say it happened because the air from Hurricane Floyd that had been moving up around the east coast of America caused large amounts of water vapour to condense into a cloud, providing a huge release of latent heat. This then drove the winds of the storm and deepened its central pressure. On 15th October at 6pm, the day before the reckoning, the depression dipped with no warning.

Earlier that week, the weather forecasts said that high winds and heavy rains were coming our way and by 15th October, the lunchtime news predicted fresh-to-strong winds of force 5-7. Nothing to really fret about. By 9.30pm, nearly ten hours later, the forecast changed quite distinctly and the wind prediction was now for a force 9-10. On the night of 16th October, when many families were tucked up in bed, the wind started to howl. It was clear that the Channel Islands were experiencing a severe gale and many people started to worry. An hour later the emergency services issued a weather warning. By midnight the storm was upon us with winds of nearly 100 mph Trees were being uprooted and thrown around. The depression had dramatically deepened to a central pressure reading of 964 millibars: it began to move north away from us along the coast of Sussex, Kent and East Anglia. At this point none of the weather forecasters had expected such a change in direction. It had developed so quickly in such a short space of time that even the experts could not predict its severity. After the storm had passed, the landscape was changed - some 15 million trees had been brought down in the UK and whole forests decimated. Buildings suffered severe damage and ships were driven onto shore. Sixteen people on the mainland died as a direct result of the storm.

In the Channel Islands it was amazing that there were no fatalities, as the winds here were at their highest. Fortunately, the stongest winds occurred in the early hours of the morning, peaking between midnight and 3am, when few people were about. Had it been during a normal working day, the death toll might have been considerable. People were advised to stay indoors but with trees blocking roads, debris falling all around, and roofs being blown off houses, this wasn't always possible.

Michael Fish makes his infamous broadcast followed by the devastation

The emergency services were overloaded with so many calls of distress that people had to wait hours for help, rather than the normal few minutes. Even then it was hard for fire-appliances, police cars and ambulances to reach their destination, as many of the roads were covered in trees and debris. Some hotels had to be evacuated for the safety of the guests, who then had to pray that nothing would fall down on top of them while they waited anxiously for assistance. It was like a war zone. Thousands of trees were brought down, amongst them all the beautiful trees at La Route Orange in St Brelade's, Jersey.

Weather forecasters, including the well-known Michael Fish, were highly criticised after the storm had settled. He had stated in an early weather report that, despite a phone call he had received from a viewer, there was not going to be a hurricane but it would be 'rather windy'. However during all the controversy, it came to people's attention that in fact the situation had been far more complex than they had realised. There had been simply no time to produce any effective data that would have enabled forecasters to observe the sudden drop in pressure and the abrupt change of direction of the storm. Michael Fish had been right: technically this had not been a hurricane, but it came close. Hurricane winds start from 120mph and can reach up to 160 mph, accompanied by much heavier rainfall than was experienced in the Great Storm. One of the outcomes of all the criticism was that the Met Office improved the way they compiled and issued severe weather warnings, making them much more prepared.

This storm, with the highest winds and level of destruction since 1703, was supposed to be a 'once in 300 years' event. Just 27 months later, on 25th January 1990, another severe storm swept across England. What can we expect in the future with the onset of global warming? Well, you know what they say: 'you can never trust the weather'.

In the Islands small planes at the airports had turned over, boats had been smashed up, thousands of trees had been brought down and hundreds of cars crushed, not to mention the damage done to buildings but luckily no one got killed. The following are just a few recollections of some people who remember that fateful night.

Trevor and Lesley Tredant (The Miramar Hotel)

I remember going to town in the afternoon and it was so still it was almost eerie. I thought 'we are in for something'. I don't remember what time high tide was but when I got back the wind was starting to pick up and getting worse. I had to go up on the roof with the barman to try to secure some rubberoid as it started flapping in the wind: that was before we knew there was a storm coming, but the wind was getting stronger and stronger. At one point I put the hammer down and it blew away so I thought 'right, that's it - it's getting too dangerous'. The wind seemed to funnel up Mont Gras d'Eau. I can't remember the time, but the roof just came off at the front and over the staff quarters and crashed down on the cars at the back. One couple must have had a hell of a shock as it came off in front of their eyes. Others at the back slept through the whole lot. We called everyone downstairs and had to evacuate them to the Silversprings Hotel up the road. A lot of them were saying 'no

ourist comforts his wife after a terrifying night in which their hotel room roof and ing were blown away

it's OK, we will stay here'. I could see the big lounge window bowing under the pressure of the wind, so I pulled the curtains and said 'Look if that window goes there will be flying glass everywhere, so let's get out now'.

I remember crouching under the reception desk to use the telephone in case the ceiling came down. The next morning we could see the devastation. Luckily no one got hurt and it was only a couple of days until the end of our season. The insurance covered us, but it took the whole winter to put things right again. I think the damage came to over £60,000 which was a lot of money in those days.

Jill Higginbotham

We used to have two jewellers' shops - Lawrence the Jeweller - in St Helier. The police phoned us to ask if we could come into town as our shop canopy was blowing up and down King Street and they were too busy to deal with it. This was about 11pm. We drove into town but at St Aubin's we got a puncture: despite everything that was going on around us, we managed to fix it. We eventually got into town and found the canopy at 11.30pm. We put it safely away down an alley beside Voisins. When we got back to our car in Broad Street, there was an empty police car and we could hear all sorts of messages coming through on the radio. One was that there was a fire engine stuck in St Peter's Valley. Driving back home along Victoria Avenue, we noticed that it was a lot windier than we had even seen it before. When we got to the bottom of Beaumont Hill, some honorary police officers said St Aubin's was closed, so we were directed up Beaumont Hill.

When we got to Les Quennevais there were more honorary police officers redirecting traffic. So we went down La Marquanderie Hill. When we got to the bottom there was another tree blocking yet another road, so we had to reverse all the way up the hill again. When we got to the top the policeman said he didn't know which way to send us as there were trees down everywhere. Eventually we managed to go down past Lloyds TSB and the Lavender Farm. When we got to the top of Mont Sohier we saw a terrible sight: a tree had come down on a small cottage.

We parked the car and managed to walk down to our house. We were in no doubt that there was something major happening! I think we stayed up until about 4am as we were worried about the house and the dogs. We eventually went to bed when we heard the storm subsiding.

In the morning I had to get back to the shop, so I went off to get the car. By now there were so many trees down everywhere that we had to climb over and under them, and my new coat was covered in green moss. When we eventually got back to the car, we were delighted to see that it hadn't been damaged. We could not move it, though, as we were blocked in. The Territorial Army was busy cutting up trees so we had to walk into town. We eventually opened the shop but closed at 12 noon as we knew nobody would be coming into town. It was one of those dramatic days when time just seemed to stand still and it took a while for it to sink in just how serious the storm had been.

Sally Bardin

We lived at La Vert Rue in St Mary's in a 200-year-old cottage. I woke in the night and tried to put on my light, but the electricity was off. I could hear a loud noise and voices so I went into the hall. It was pitch black. My sister was already in the hall: I don't know how but we bumped into each other and I bashed her in the face with my head. She had a big bruise in the morning. We could hear lots of things falling over in the loft and a screaming wind outside. We all went into the lounge. My sister said she was going to go outside and see what was happening. I said 'Don't you dare go out there'. It is hard to describe the noise. I have never heard anything like it before in my life. She didn't listen to me and went outside. I was so frightened, I screamed and screamed because I thought something bad was going to happen to her as it was just going mental out there.

She soon came back in and said 'you are not going to believe this but the roof is moving'. Now you have to bear in mind that this roof is massive. I mean, if I was standing in the loft I could have got four people on my shoulders. That's how high the roof was. I could hear our cockerel screeching outside, so me and my sister went out to the hen-house. It had rolled over two or three times and the cockerel was trapped in the wire. All the chickens had disappeared ... probably got blown away. We freed him and ran back with him into the house.

All I can remember is the banging and banging. I looked across at Dad and said 'we've got to get out of this house'. 'I know, I know, but where?' he replied. I said 'I don't know but we got to get out now', as I was sure that something would come through the roof and we would all be killed. There was a massive oak tree outside and it might have fallen on the house.

We did not know where to go, so we decided to get into the car. The wind was so loud that I was screaming at my sister and she was saying 'What? What? I can't hear you'. We tried to drive to my brother's house, but each road we took, there were trees down. We were trapped. So we drove into a field near our house and parked out of the way of the trees and waited for the storm to pass, which seemed to take forever.

When it had quietened down a bit, my mum said 'Look at your dad, he is in shock. Can you go back to the house and get the bottle of whisky which I keep for emergencies?' So my sister and I went back to the house. When we got there, my sister said 'Oh my God, look at the house'. It did not look like our home; it looked like something out of a horror film and I remember thinking that this could not be real and that I would wake up in a minute. The whole roof had come off. I don't know when it had happened, but it must have been minutes after we left the house. If we had been there, God knows what would have happened to us as the roof landed just where we had been standing earlier. We all eventually went back home and sat in the lounge, which was open to the sky. Something made me jump as I heard 'cock a doodle doo' and the cockerel crawled out from behind the sofa. It must have been there all night. We all just sat there completely shell-shocked.

My brother came around and we tried to clear up and put some plastic over the roof, but as we were working, it poured with rain and everything got ruined - beds, carpets everything!

It really did knock my dad for six, especially when the insurance man came round and said we were not covered, as it was an Act of God. My parents had been paying their premiums for over 25 years and didn't get a penny back, they just couldn't believe it.

A local builder helped us out in the end called Hayden Lister, he was brilliant, he said just pay me when you can. My sister and I had been working since we were 17 so we had some savings and both put our money together to help out.

I remember once later saying to my dad 'You know you said I will always have a roof over my head? Well, maybe it will have to be in the garden'. That was the only time we managed to make him smile about it.

The roof is completely ripped off Sallys' parent's granite cottage

This photo from a helicopter shows a roof is also ripped off this block of fla
Mont Millais

Note the three bedrooms from different flats

Chapter Eight

The Gasworks Fire

When we think of a fire at a gasworks, we imagine huge explosions and devastation for miles around. Buildings exploding, cars and houses being destroyed: it all sounds a little like something you would see in a movie. It is not exactly 'good television' if the cavalry ride in and save the day when we had been expecting some dramatic action. Hollywood is not real life - when film crews burn down the set, it can be rebuilt in a matter of hours, and of course the buildings are empty, so no-one gets hurt.

Imagine now what St Helier would be like in the wake of such a disaster: if the town, home to so many of our shops and businesses, had been wiped out with a death toll counted in the thousands. On 19th March 1982 this could easily have been the outcome, if our own fire service and gas company employees had not acted so quickly.

Around 12.40 in the afternoon a tanker was being unloaded into one of the massive butane storage spheres, when gas began to escape. It set off a warning alarm and the fire brigade was called. When they began an attempt to contain the leak, there was a sudden flash as the gas ignited and created a huge fireball. A reporter who was filming at the scene saw two men caught by the blast, one receiving serious injuries to his hands and face. So strong was the heat that in places the fireman's protective clothing simply melted.

As the seriousness of the situation became clear, every policeman was rushed to the scene of the accident. This was not as easy as it sounds: Chief Inspector Arthur Le Maistre said that when the alarm was raised, there had not been enough officers available at police headquarters: more had to be called in from around the Island and those just finishing a shift were asked to stay on. Fearful of public safety, the police sealed off a large area around the gasworks. Houses and small shops were evacuated, and even the Honorary Police were called out to help with traffic diversions. Quite soon the town centre stood as still as a ghost town. Every road in the vicinity of the explosion was cordoned off. Such a widespread evacuation was necessary because, in emptying the tanker, a second leak had been discovered. Controlling the emergency was made more difficult because none of the emergency services or gasworks staff were allowed to communicate by radio, as a single spark might have caused an explosion. The police followed a well-rehearsed, pre-determined plan for such an incident, including putting the hospital on full alert.

The fire service later admitted that they had been terrified that the two large gas butane storage spheres would explode, causing a massive blast that would have devastated much of the surrounding residential area. They said that such a situation was simply "too frightening to contemplate". It was potentially the most dangerous incident with which the fire service in Jersey has ever had to deal with.

By 2pm, almost two hours after the alarm, the fire service had the blaze under control. A spokesman for the station said that their main priority had been to spray water over the surface of the tanks to cool them down, then to put out the flames. If they had concentrated only on the fire, the leak could have become much worse, with severe consequences.

Around the same time, the hospital said that nine people had been injured, amongst them two firemen and three gas company employees. Fire service deputy chief officer Brian Mallet and fireman Malcolm Bouchere were the two men who had been badly hurt when hit by the fireball. There were fears for a third fireman who was believed to have jumped into a water tank to escape the blast, but police divers found no-one and the man was later discovered in another area, uninjured. One gas company employee was so severely burnt that people said he had lost all his hair, and the skin on his hands was coming off in strips. The final injury count was 10 men, three of whom were airlifted to Odstock, an English hospital which specialises in severe burns. One of the men, Tom Hannah (63), was seriously injured, but his son said that he had been well enough to talk to him. Defence Committee president Senator John Ellis was full of praise for the work done by the firemen and also by the staff who suffered injuries dealing with an emergency greater than any of them had ever seen before.

When the incident was over (for those involved it must have seemed like the longest two hours of their lives) the main feeling was one of relief. The biggest worry had been that the gas cloud leaking from the tanker could have ignited the two huge butane gas spheres, which would have destroyed much of St Helier. As the gasworks is in a densely populated residential area - something that has since been brought into question - the death toll could have been horrendous. Next day, investigations began to look for the cause of the accident and two inspectors from the UK Health and Safety Executive arrived.

Amid all the commotion of putting the fire out, there was a good deal of worry and panic on the streets of St Helier as the news spread. In the Wellington Bar a Mrs Kellet had heard the bangs caused by the explosion, but thought it was thunder until a neighbour told her to evacuate her house. On the other hand Shirley Murray, who lived down the road by the Temple, slept through it all as she had been working a night-shift and had not realised what had gone on. Despite the worry and confusion, the evacuees stuck together and helped one another out in their time of need.

This is another of those stories where I have to end by praising the workers who helped to save so many lives. In a situation like this where thousands could have died, I think we should be praising them every day and recognise the job they do and the dangers they face. They saved part of the parish from near-extinction and ensured no-one died. The only people injured were those who were helping: they risked their own lives for the many people of St Helier.

Gasworks

ou can imagine by this picture the devastation that could have occurred if the gas lding tanks had exploded

Chapter Nine

The Newall Murders

This story is of a sadistic nature. Many have heard of the brother who murdered his parents, and the other brother who helped cover up his awful crime. To the younger generation, it has taken on the quality of a legend: just driving through Grève de Lecq gives you an eerie feeling because of all those tales heard in childhood. Stories can be embroidered, or have bits left out - and most of the time we use our imaginations to fill in the gaps. No-one apart from Roderick Newall will ever know the full story but, using my research, I am going to piece it together and tell as much of the truth as I can.

The father was Nicholas Newall. He had aspirations to become a writer of children's stories and had written at least two manuscripts but had not found a publisher. Nicholas had a twin brother Stephen, the spitting image of him, who was later to play a major role in uncovering the truth. They were never poor but neither did they consider themselves to be a rich family - they just knew they were 'well off.' Nicholas and his brother were given half a million pounds by their Uncle Kenneth: they already owned a house in Spain and a yacht, which sounds about right for people with enough money to do what they please. The irony of it was that Nicholas' family and friends said he was very careful about managing his money and did not like to spend a fortune on anything. Others have said that he did not like to see any money wasted. When talking about sailing, he often came across as arrogant and domineering, but in a domestic situation he was withdrawn and in many ways incompetent. Many people found Nicholas to be arrogant on first meeting, but this often meant that he simply didn't want to know you.

Elizabeth Newall seemed immature compared to Nicholas, perhaps because she liked to have fun and he was so up-tight, or perhaps the strictness of her husband brought out her childlike side. An active woman, she had been a physical education instructor and loved sports. She could be quick-witted and a good thinker, but people said that - like Nicholas - she had little interest in domestic matters. Elizabeth had always been keenly interested in the stock market and took great pleasure in following her stocks and shares. Nicholas criticised her stock-market dealing and, at one point, handed over the management of his financial affairs to his younger son Mark, giving him power of attorney over their assets and bank accounts while Nicholas spent considerable amounts of time in Spain. He seemed to have more faith in Mark's abilities than he did in Elizabeth's.

To close friends the Newalls seemed larger than life because everything they did was pushed to the limit: they drove their cars fast and they drank hard.

Both Nicholas and Elizabeth came from wealthy families. As they were both teachers it is no surprise that they met and fell in love at work, at New Park School, St Andrew's. They were married on 20th December 1963 in Scotland and two years later they were graced with their first child, Roderick Innes Nelson, who was born on 11th April 1965 in Glasgow. Just over a year later along came Mark Stephen Nelson on 22nd

June 1966. This I feel is when the roller coaster began its climb to the top, unsuspecting of the fall in years to come.

In the late 60s Nicholas and Elizabeth, both keen and experienced sailors, left their professions and bought a yacht. They realised that if they took care of their money they would be able to live comfortably without having to work for a living. While sailing towards the West Indies, the family made a stop in Jersey to pick up a nanny for the two boys. Unfortunately after a few days on the water, the nanny was taken ill and they had to turn around and head back to the Island. During their pit-stop Nicholas and Elizabeth began to explore and Nicholas was entranced by the the fact that Jersey had its own parliament, its legal system and even its welcome tax laws. In that moment he decided that this was his place to be and they would go no further with their sailing.

Their first house was Martello Lodge at St Brelade's Bay, but they did not stay long, moving in 1972 to their new home the Crow's Nest overlooking Grève de Lecq bay. Even though they seemed settled, in 1977 Nicholas bought a further house in Spain where they spent several months at a time sailing the blue waters. Back in Jersey Nicholas got a teaching job at St Michael's school, where Roderick and Mark attended. Elizabeth took a small supply teaching job, but her real energies went into her love of competitive sports and she became a keen tennis player - always out to win.

The two sons were brought up in a strict parental regime and supervised by a nanny. Nicholas and Elizabeth were always careful in their choice of schools for the boys, as they wanted the best education for them. St Michael's was a highly respected school because of the quality of the teachers and the way in which the children were encouraged to learn. When Roderick was seven and Mark six, they were sent away to an English boarding school - Lockers Park Preparatory at Hemel Hempstead in Hertfordshire. To be full boarders at this tender age was unusual and most pupils from St Michael's didn't transfer to a boarding school until they were nine or even 13. Six years later Roderick and Mark transferred to Radley College at Abingdon in Oxfordshire. Here they remained until they were 18.

Nicholas set very high standards for his sons. As well as instilling a 'love of learning', he encouraged them to take part in sports and outdoor activities. People around the Newalls saw no reason for any worries about the children's upbringing. The boys were very keen surfers and were introduced to skiing, scuba diving, golf, sailing and water-skiing at an early age. Other reports said that even though the brothers were not unloved, they did not feel needed. At times they were treated coldly, especially by their father, who rarely showed them any affection. Nicholas would not even give up time to play with them, and always referred to them as Elizabeth's boys. He rarely participated in the activities in which the boys were encouraged to take part. As a family they were four very individual people with volatile natures.

Roderick was always bigger than Mark and seemed to dominate his brother. They did come together through one bond: one that many victims share. Because of the force of their father's personality, they struggled to find their own identity or to build any form of relationship with their parents. This bond was strong and their loyalty to each other from within was very deep. On the outside, it was a different story. They were continuously in competition and would fight regularly - so much so that when they were studying at Radley the boys had to be sent home separately on holidays.

Both brothers felt neglected, but it was Mark who seemed to feel the most keen sense of rejection. He hid these feelings under a hard exterior. Mark became head boy, but was not hugely popular. Fellow students said that Mark was arrogant and unpleasant to be around. On many occasions he would have fits of anger, punching his fists through the plaster walls. At other times he would walk around the school with a leather strap wrapped around his knuckles. Mark felt that he was going to be attacked by the older pupils, as had happened when he first arrived.

Roderick Newall covered up any feelings of neglect and living a loveless life by doing the opposite of his brother. He became a leader whom people would follow; a daredevil who would thrive on attention. He became an NCO in Radley's own cadet force, which helped him achieve his main ambition: to join the army. He told his friends that it was because he wanted to 'kill people.' I would have found this slightly unnerving, but he was just a young lad and boys always seem to enjoy wanting to blow up things. Teachers took pride in the parent/pupil relationship and said that it would help build team spirit. Many of the parents would visit and watch their children participate in sporting competitions. On one occasion Nicholas arrived to watch Roderick in a race. Being so distant from the boys, he was unable to recognize Roderick and pointed his video camera at the wrong boy. What was even worse was that when Nicholas discovered his mistake he just simply handed over the video tape to the parents of the boy he had filmed, and did not even mention to Roderick the mistake which he had made.

Mark and Roderick were both highly intelligent and capable, intellectually and physically. Roderick went on to fulfil his dream as an army officer and Mark went into fund management. They had promising futures ahead of them. Roderick soon found the army to be too much like home and when his uncle made the brothers a substantial cash gift, it was the chance for Roderick to take another look at his life. His dreams of travel could become a reality. Mark's career on the other hand was going extremely well. For a man who was only 20, he was set up for life with a satisfying job as a Eurobond dealer working for the Banque Arabe et Internationale d'Investissments. Mark was very bright and, unlike his brother, saw an excellent future in his chosen career in which he took great pride and pleasure.

There are many more stories about the brothers' lives and you can find out more in a couple of books which have been written about them. I think this is enough to set out their background, which can be viewed either as strict parenting and neglected boys, or 'tough love' parents who only wanted the best for their children. Here is where the story fast-forwards to 10th October 1987.

It was the evening of Friday 9th October, when both Roderick and Mark arrived in the Island as a birthday surprise for their mother Elizabeth. Roderick stayed at his brother's new house from where they phoned their parents to say that they were going to take them out for dinner the following evening. It is said that Roderick also implied that he wanted to talk about money and the future. Elizabeth seemed excited that the boys were coming over before she and Nicholas went to Spain later that month.

On Saturday 10th October Roderick and Mark arrived as planned at their parents' house. Mark and his father went out again immediately to pick up a van they had hired to take some furniture to Mark's house. This would be the vehicle that would later transport Nicholas and Elizabeth's bodies. At 8pm at Clos de L'Atlantique, the Newalls started their celebrations with two expensive bottles of champagne. An hour or so later they moved to the Sea Crest restaurant to dine. During their meal another bottle of champagne was consumed as well as wine and liqueurs. Just after midnight the family returned to Elizabeth and Nicholas's home where they switched to whisky. Like many of us when we drink, our tongues loosen and we gain the confidence to speak our minds. With Uncle Kenneth's money on Roderick's mind, it was also apparent that there was a tense atmosphere, as childhood feelings began to surface about his parents' loveless rules, boarding school, and even the army. Through a statement from Mark made in 1994 we know that an argument broke out about Roderick's career. Mark said he had heard most of this before and, being sober, he just went home and left them to get on with it. This time, however, it allegedly became a violent confrontation between father and son.

At one point they were standing nose-to-nose, and each let rip about the way they felt about each other over the years, saying things that had never been said before. Nicholas pushed Roderick which resulted in him hitting his head on the dining room table where just hours before they were happily sipping drinks. In retaliation, Roderick reached for a box that he had earlier taken down from the attic. On top was a pair of rice flails

- a weapon used in martial arts. Roderick used these to club his father around the head, then fell to the ground himself. All went blank. His next memory was finding himself on the floor staring into the eyes of his dead father. He went to check on his mother. No pulse. As the realisation hit him that he had killed both of his parents, he felt an overwhelming sense of despair. Among the bloody carnage, Roderick phoned his brother telling him what he had done. He also told Mark that the only thing he could do was to take his own life as well.

Mark later described the phone call in his statement and how Roderick, though incoherent, admitted to killing both their parents. Mark went around to the house. Here he found his parents' bodies covered in blood. His brother was also covered in blood, crying and in a very distressed state, holding his father's shotgun. Mark told Roderick to phone the police but Roderick kept talking about shooting himself. The police would not understand, he said. Eventually the decision was made that Mark would help to conceal the murders. If he had not done this, says Mark, then he was sure Roderick would have killed himself.

All over the rooms there were splatters of blood, almost like a butcher's shop. This needed to be cleaned before morning. Because of the amount of time that the bodies had been on the floor, the blood had drained from Nicholas' open skull and been soaked into the carpet. Elizabeth was believed to have fallen to her knees after the first blow and would have probably died in that very position. In the bedroom there were specks of blood on the lampshade and the blood had even soaked its way through the parquet flooring. Mark went to find something to hide the bodies in. On searching the garage, garden shed and boiler room he found some tarpaulins, tools and various other pieces of equipment to clean and dispose of any evidence. They wrapped their parents' bodies in the tarpaulin and carefully put them into the back of the van they had hired a few days before. Their destination for the burial of the bodies was near Grève de Lecq, where as young boys they used to play. They removed the corpses from the van and rolled them over the bank. Together the brothers then dug a shallow grave that was 2 feet 3 inches deep. It has been suggested in one report that the bodies of Nicholas and Elizabeth were buried on top of each other in a head-to-toe position. Mark and Roderick then returned to the house. Daylight was already upon them. Stains were scrubbed and scrubbed, but still remained visible on the bedroom floor. To ensure that everything would dry quickly, they turned up the central heating.

That morning at 8:45am a close friend of Elizabeth, Maureen Ellam, arrived at the house with a bouquet of flowers. Roderick answered and said that his parents were still asleep. Maureen was a little suspicious, wondering why they were still in bed, but decided to leave the flowers for Roderick to give to his mother.

Later on Roderick burnt some of his parents' possessions close to the old Newall family home at Grève de Lecq. It was here on March 8th 1988, almost five months later, that police dogs found the debris and traced the belongings back to Nicholas and Elizabeth Newall.

In his initial statement Roderick claimed that he returned to his parents' house after the meal and it was late. They opened a bottle of whisky and had an extra couple of drinks. A few hours

Nicholas and Elizabeth Newall and the woods in which their bodies were buried

The Newall's family home 'The Crow's Nest' at Grève de Lecq

later he and Mark left in the van to go back to Mark's house. When he left, his parents were preparing to go to bed. Next morning he said that he went with Mark and entered the house via the back door. There was no sign of activity, so they assumed their parents were still asleep after a heavy night of drinking. After checking on their parents and finding them asleep, they both went to the kitchen to make some breakfast. At roughly 9am Roderick heard the doorbell and went to the door where a woman, who he later learned was Mrs Ellam, gave him the flowers. He then said that his parents awoke, but there was minimal conversation going on, so he and Mark both left to run an errand for their father - collecting an old mattress in the van. This chore done, Roderick said they then arrived back just before midday and sat down for lunch at around 12:30pm. During the meal, accompanied by a couple of bottles of wine, the topic of conversation again was the money being given to the boys from Uncle Kenneth. At 3pm, Roderick and Mark said they had to go to catch their flights back to England. So they off-loaded the mattress, returned the hire van to Falles Hire Cars at the airport, and by 5:45pm Roderick was on a plane. Unsurprisingly Mark Newall's statement was exactly the same. Knowing what we know now, the statements must have surely seemed suspicious as they each remembered exact times.

As the brothers were making their journey home, they were the only two people in the world who knew what each other had done, and that neither they (nor anyone else) would ever see their parents again. Their bodies would not be found for years to come.

It was Maureen Ellam who first began to show concern as it was unusual of her friends not to call: they were always having a chat on the phone. Maureen had not heard from Elizabeth Newall for two days and was curious and worried about what she was doing. Her first thought was that they had gone over to Sark to see Kenneth. However one of her main concerns was that they could be in trouble due to the great storm, which occurred on 16th October. Perhaps their house had been damaged as roofs were coming off and trees falling down all around the area. She even began to think that they could be seriously hurt. On managing to convince her husband to go over to their house, their suspicions arose. David Ellam found a pile of unopened mail, the living room neater than it was usually, and the central heating on full blast. A wet dressing gown was outside on the slab. David didn't think anything of it because it had probably been hung out to dry. He found Mark's number and rang him. The call went straight to Mark's answer machine. Eventually they contacted Roderick who returned a few days later, and went to the house where he was accompanied by Mrs Ellam. She regrets now that she pointed out some of the odd things around the house that she'd noticed, because Roderick immediately put these straight, thus potentially jeopardising the investigation. Little did she know that the man walking around the family home with her was the murderer.

The Newalls were reported missing and a massive hunt got underway. The police searched the house and questioned the brothers, but with no other witnesses, the house seemingly in order and their statements matching, it was hard for them to build a case. Many said that the couple may have just left the Island for their house in Spain, but that also drew a blank as none of their friends there had seen them either. Eventually the police sent in a forensic team to examine the house.

This showed a different picture altogether. With the help of ultra-violet lights they found traces of numerous blood stains that had not quite been cleaned away and a murder hunt was launched.

Further crucial evidence was later discovered around the Island. The police found some upholstery cleaner with a brush attachment, embedded in which were tufts of fibre, which forensic analysis showed was a match for the carpets in both the lounge and bedrooms. Partially burnt and melted tarpaulins were found, the same type and colour that had been sold in Norman's store on 10th October 1987. Fibres were also found in pieces of green and white J-cloths. A spade was discovered buried in the undergrowth at Noirmont Common identical to the spade that was bought from Norman's the day before the murders. However, there was still no evidence to connect Roderick and Mark with the crime and the brothers protested their innocence and of course they did not have the DNA technology of today.

Roderick travelled to Spain on his family's 66ft yacht and cruised around the Mediterranean while back at home the investigation continued. He was doing what he liked to do best, - sail. Would this help him forget the awful images he had in his head of the horrific murder he had performed? Knowing the police could not contact him, he decided to set sail to the Falkland Islands, where he dreamt of a yacht-chartering business. At only 23 Roderick had plenty of time to come up with a plan to evade capture, and try to begin a new life.

Around two years later, on 19th December 1989, police investigations came to a halt and Elizabeth and Nicholas' home was given back to the family, redecorated and cleaned. No-one had heard anything from the two brothers for almost a year. Mark was in New York and Roderick was preparing to set up his yacht chartering business.

In 1991 Mark phoned Roderick to tell him that their parents had been officially declared dead and that the brothers were going to inherit a fortune. At this time Roderick was in Brazil where he had met a women called Elena Pedo and had told her he had just become a millionaire. He sold his yacht and in January 1992 flew with Elena to Miami to look for a new one. One night, when they had been out to see a movie, the scenes of violence in it seem to have triggered Roderick's need to confess. He did not tell the police, he told Elena. She did not believe him.

Many felt that Roderick had longed to confess all to his father's twin brother Stephen and the police saw an opportunity in this. When Roderick came to England in the summer of 1992, on another yacht-buying trip, he drove up to see his grandmother in Scotland. Roderick was put under surveillance and police set up a meeting between him and Stephen at the Dunkeld House Hotel. They bugged the room and briefed Stephen not to press for a confession. When Roderick arrived, the two men had a general chat about what they'd been doing recently. During the conversation Roderick confessed, but in a way that was so cryptic that it would have been hard for any witness to describe exactly what he had said. His sentences tailed off and though the inference was clear, the words he used didn't really make sense, but it was a confession. From this they learned that the bodies were in plastic and had been camouflaged, and that Roderick carried the blame along with someone else. If the police moved in, he said, he had a suicide pact with his accomplice. On listening to his nephew, Stephen could hear what a struggle it had been for Roderick over these past few years. He could also see that a huge burden had been lifted from Roderick's shoulders.

Despite the confession, the Scottish police were not able to arrest Roderick immediately. They had to wait for a warrant from Jersey where the director of prosecutions, who had been working on this case for the last five years, was worried that the tape recording might not be enough evidence to take to a jury. He needed to hear the tape for himself. This gave Roderick a good head start. While driving on the M6 Roderick knew he was being tailed, so he made good use of his army training and gave his pursuers the slip. Telling family members he was unable to visit them, he made his way to the South of France to collect his boat, but the law was hot on his heels: two days later on 17th July a warrant was issued for his arrest. At the time Mark was working in Paris, but police learned he had plans to meet his brother in Tangiers at the end of the month. It was to be their last face-to-face meeting for 15 months - the next time they saw each other would be in La Moye Prison.

In the end it took the Royal Navy to stop Roderick, by intercepting his yacht 150 miles southwest of Gibraltar. He had been heading for the Falkland Islands via the Canaries. His mistake had been to fly the Red Ensign, which enabled the Royal Navy to stop him - had he been flying a Spanish or French flag, they would have had no authority to detain him. Once aboard Roderick was told to put his hands up: he refused. He was told to lie on the floor: he refused. The officers then showed him the Jersey warrant. On 7th August 1992 Roderick Newall was arrested for the murder of Elizabeth and Nicholas Newall - nearly five years after the brutal, bloody murders had happened.

Roderick was not returned to Jersey straight away, and remained in the custody of the Gibraltar police. He would be able to return to Jersey if the evidence against him was not challenged. If this happened, then it could take up to a year to bring him back to the Island. While on remand, he was able to follow the news and read the papers, allowing him to assess the attitudes of the investigators and their evidence. The police and reporters believed that it was a good idea to keep the investigation open to the public eye, as they thought the publicity would help. Roderick went on a hunger strike but it only lasted four days - it was suggested that he had been upset by the refusal of his bail application.

On 17th December with Roderick still in remand, the police had managed to track down Mark and arrest him. He was detained in Paris' main prison, La Sante. It appeared that the extradition would be a lot easier than Roderick's. However on hearing the news about his brother, Roderick attempted suicide, using a syringe that had been hidden in an orange. He soon recovered. Mark eventually arrived back in the Island on 30th April 1993 in a chartered jet. That evening he was charged with murder. On 4th May Mark pleaded not guilty to the murder of his parents. It wasn't until 5th November that the Governor of Gibraltar signed a warrant for Roderick's extradition. The following day at 7:30am Roderick was on his way back to Jersey. When in the air Roderick was accompanied by his advocate, who handed the Assistant Chief Officer, Paul Marks, a map of Jersey. On closer inspection he saw that Roderick had indicated where the graves of his parents were. A larger scale map was then given to Roderick to mark more precisely the location of the bodies.

Once in the Island Roderick was charged with the murder of his parents. Later that day Roderick accompanied the police to the location of his parents' graves. It was only 500 yards away from the old house. Now, just over six years later, the landscape had changed dramatically due to the great storm, and Roderick found it difficult to pinpoint the exact spot. The bodies were not to be found that day or the next. The search was now concentrating on a corner of field, suggested by Roderick. During the excavation they discovered black polythene lying in a shallow trench. On examination, it was found to contain Nicholas Newall's shoe and foot. His body was discovered in a green tarpaulin, and the remains of Elizabeth's was discovered in a blue one. Even though this had not been unexpected, police found themselves in shock. How could this happen in an Island so small? The ambulance arrived to take the bodies: as they did so, the police took off their helmets in a mark of respect.

It was later recognised that the Newalls had died from severe head injuries made by a blunt weapon. The most severe wounds that Nicholas had suffered were on the back of his head, from a sharp-edged weapon. One thing that did make the forensic team curious was that phenobarbitone was found in the stomachs of Elizabeth and Nicholas. Phenobarbitone is used for people suffering from epilepsy and neither of the Newalls were sufferers. The drug's side-effects can include drowsiness and even sedation.

On Monday 8th August 1994, the Royal Court was filled with police officers and media reporters. Roderick and Mark were both led into the court. Finally justice would be served and the grim reality of the brothers' impending loss of freedom was clear in the paleness of their faces. As well as their freedom, they were to be stripped of their inheritance. The court agreed that the evidence showed this had not been a spontaneous crime and that it was well thought out. Roderick Newall was given a double life sentence; Mark was sentenced to six years for helping cover up the murders. When they were escorted away they displayed no sign of emotion.

Mark served a 20 month sentence and after fighting an earlier judgment was allegedly able to get his inheritance restored. Roderick was released from prison in 2007 after serving 12 years and it is has been reported that he now lives in the UK working as an IT tutor.

Chapter Ten

Occupation Tragedies

War and tragedy go hand-in-hand and there are many shocking stories I could tell you of the German Occupation of the Channel Islands. It is a fascinating subject: we were the only part of Britain to be occupied by the Germans during World War Two and for five long years the Swastika flew here in place of the Union Jack. Along with the worst aspects of Nazi rule came the propaganda. The photograph of the *Luftwaffe* burying RAF pilots on British soil with full military honours is one of a number that shocked the Islands and the world. The Germans clearly thought the Islands were just stepping-stones to England. Here are three short stories about those dark days of the Occupation.

François Scornet

When General Charles de Gaulle made an impassioned plea for men and women to form a Free French force to help the fight against Germany, young François Scornet was quick to respond. De Gaulle's plea had come in a radio broadcast made from England in December 1940. The war was well underway: Germany had invaded Poland and then marched into France. On 5th June 1940, the French Prime Minister Paul Reynaud had appointed Charles de Gaulle as his Minister of War, but had been ousted as premier by Marshal Henri-Philippe Petain. Instead of fighting Germany, Petain wanted to seek an armistice. De Gaulle worried that he would be arrested if he stayed in France, so he fled to England and it was from there that he made the radio appeal. On 13th December 1940, 16 young Frenchmen, including 21-year-old François Scornet, set sail from France to England in an open boat. They were all young cadets: their aim was to reach England to join De Gaulle's Free French forces, which one day would liberate their homeland.

The crossing was rough and their navigational systems were destroyed. For hour after hour they found themselves sailing around not knowing where they were. As they approached a coast which they assumed to be the Isle of Wight, they came ashore, not knowing that in fact it was German-occupied Guernsey. They jumped off onto the beach and began to sing the Marseillaise. To their astonishment they were captured by the Germans and sent for interrogation. Because the German Command Headquarters was in Jersey, six men were sent there for trial. François Scornet, who then admitted being the ringleader, was condemned to death and was held at the Grand Hotel under a heavy guard. On 17th March 1941 in the early hours of the morning, German officers called upon Reverend Pere Mare, a Roman Catholic priest from St Thomas' Church. They told him that François was due to be shot later that morning and so needed to receive his last rites. At 5.00am Rev Pere Mare went to see François where he administered communion. François ' shooting was designed to send a loud and clear message to the local population that turning against Germany would not be tolerated. François was allowed to write one last letter to his parents in which he said "I believe the end of my existence has come, I will die for France, bravely facing the enemy. In an hour it will be finished...be assured that I will die a good Christian... for the last time I embrace you".

Later that morning Scornet was taken on a lorry, alongside his own coffin, the firing squad and the priest to St Ouen's Manor, where he was tied to a tree and executed by a German military firing squad at 8.20am. When the undertaker arrived to remove the body it had already been left for more than nine hours, still tied to the tree. Some time after François ' death, the tree was struck by lightning and a piece of its wood was used to make a crucifix which is used by the deacons of St Thomas' church to this day. Four years after his execution, and two months after the liberation of the Island, François Scornet's remains were exhumed from Almorah cemetery and taken to a private chapel. His body was then returned to his home town of Plougean in France. A ceremony was also held at St Thomas' church in his honour, which was overflowing with people. An annual memorial service for François Scornet is held at St Ouen's Manor.

Henry Peter Turpin

On 1st February 1941 around 11pm, a 29-year-old was shot and killed by a German sentry. Henry Peter Turpin was shot dead on La Grande Route des Mielles, also known as the Five Mile Road. He was in the military zone just outside his home in St Ouen. These military zones were very restricting and no resident living within a zone was allowed to be out and about after 8pm. This curfew lasted until 7.30am the next morning. People also had to carry green identification cards issued by the Connétable of the Parish.

Henry Peter Turpin broke the curfew, leaving the home of his friend Mr Bougeard a little before 11pm, to walk to his own house just 50 yards up the road. He was approached and

BEKANNTMACHUNG:

FRANÇOIS SCORNET,
geb. 25-5-1919, zuletzt wohnhaft in
Ploujean (Departement Finistere) ist

PUBLICATION:

The population is herewith notified, that
FRANÇOIS SCORNET,
born on May 25th 1919, residing in
Ploujean (Department Finistere) has
been sentenced

TO DEATH

by the German War Court and has
been shot on March 17th, 1941. This
had to be done, because of his favouring
the actions of the enemy by wilfully
supporting England in the war against
the German Empire.

German War Court.
March 23rd, 1941.

The notice that informed the public of the execution, François and a German Militar
Firing Squad

140

challenged by a German army sentry on patrol. At that moment Henry panicked: perhaps he had forgotten his ID card, or was worried about what might happen. So he made a run for it. 'Halt!' shouted the officer, but Henry ignored him. The sentry opened fire and the rifle's bullet struck Henry straight on the shoulder, killing him. His young son, who was only seven at the time, remembers finding his father's dead body, lying on its back in front of their garage. Because of the curfew nothing could be done until the following morning. It was one more lesson for the local population.

Louisa Gould

Louisa Gould, who lived in St Ouen, was only one of seven people in the Island to be arrested on the grounds of harbouring slave workers, an action motivated by genuine compassion. This occurred in the late spring of 1944. This is a story about how one woman helped the people who were being transported around the world like herds of cattle, confined to disgusting living-spaces, poorly fed, and falling to pieces both mentally and physically. Louisa Gould's crime, if you can call it that, was that for 20 months she hid a Russian slave worker who had managed to escape in 1942 from a Nazi camp. Louisa believed that, even though the local population was suffering enormous hardships, this did not give them the right to ignore the needs of those who were seen as 'worthless'.

Louisa's father, a seaman, was born in Brittany but emigrated to Jersey. He had nine children, Louisa being born in Jersey on 7th October 1891. Widowed before the Occupation, she ran Millais Stores, a general store at La Fontaine, St Ouen. Louisa had two well-educated boys, but lost one in July 1941 to the war. Eighteen months later, she was asked by somebody to shelter Feoder ('Bill') Burryi. It turned out that 'Bill' was a fugitive Russian, and was looking for a safe place to hide. Lousia felt it was her obligation to prevent another mother from losing her son, and took Bill under her wing.

Bill Burryi was born in 1919 to a Smolensk family who were extremely poor. When he was a young child the family moved to Tomsk in Siberia. Bill did well at school. He was a keen photographer and won a place to study for a year in Moscow. When the Nazis invaded the Soviet Union, Bill was called to serve in the airforce, but his plane was shot down. As he parachuted to the ground, he realised he was about to land in an area encircled by Germans. After just five days he was taken prisoner and sent to Jersey as a slave worker as the Germans needed such labour here to construct the many bunkers and fortifications around the Islands. One day he managed to escape.

Louisa looked after Bill for 20 months: it would have been for longer had it not been for an anonymous letter denouncing her. The letter was addressed to 'German Feldkommandantur', but a slight mistake in the address meant it was delivered to Victoria College rather than Victoria College House. There, it landed on the desk of Pat Tatam who was the Vice Principal of the College who steamed open the letter. On reading what it said, he sealed it again and sent a bicycle messenger out to warn Louisa that she was in danger. Bill immediately left and was given refuge at another house while Louisa tried to removed every trace of his having been there. In her hurry, however, she was not thorough enough: the Germans found a camera, a radio, and Christmas gifts addressed to Bill. Straight away she was arrested and entered prison on 25th May 1944.

Louisa was charged with failure to surrender a wireless receiving apparatus and giving assistance to an escaped Russian prisoner of war. On 29th June 1944, she was deported along with 18 other Jersey prisoners, to a jail in France. Later she was sent on to the Ravensbruck concentration camp, just north of Berlin. It was here in February 1945 that Louisa Gould perished in one of the most dreadful inventions of the war:- a gas chamber. After all she had done to help a man in need, just for having a few pieces of equipment such as a camera she died in the most horrific way. How lucky we are now as a nation to be allowed to do all we want. We are indeed fortunate and should remember to respect the generation that suffered so much for us.

In This House
Mrs Louisa Mary Gould,
née Le Druillenec,
Sheltered An Escaped Russian P.O.W.
During The German Occupation
From October 1942 Until May 1944.
After Her Arrest She Was
Deported To The Concentration
Camp At Ravensbruck
Where She Perished
In The Gas Chamber.

Louisa and the plaque that hangs on her old house today

Chapter Eleven

The Dakota Crash

In Jersey we very rarely see any serious plane crashes. We hear on the odd occasion that a plane has to be diverted when there is trouble landing, due to weather or technical problems, but these never result in a death. On April 14th 1965 a tragic plane crash occurred. This was the first serious accident since 1938, which meant that Jersey had had a clean slate for 27 years.

In the early evening of 14th April, a Dakota plane attempted to land at Jersey's airport at 7pm. Amid the thick fog and low-lying mist, the aircraft struck a landing pole. Further along it hit a tree at Oak Walk in St Peter's, only 400 yards from the eastern end of the runway. It then overturned and cart-wheeled into a ploughed field. Here it burst into flames. It was a harrowing sight to see the wreckage and carnage spread across the field. The plane had landed on its back and had been completely torn apart, with only the tail end still intact.

Captain Peter CE Self, a Guernsey man with a wife and young son, was piloting the plane. As it took off from Orly Airport in Paris at 5.32pm it was already 15 minutes behind schedule. Also on board the Dakota were the plane's first officer J. Lockhart-Mure, second officer H, Greenway, airhostess Dominique Sillère, and 23 passengers. Amongst the passengers, many were arriving ready for the holiday season to start work in the hotels, so there were French, Italian and Portuguese people as well as men and women from Jersey and Guernsey.

When the plane began its descent, Captain Self must have struggled to find his way through the fog without all the technical equipment that aircraft carry today, such as GPS. The mist was thick and was creeping across the runway as in an eerie graveyard in a horror film. Onlookers saw the Dakota suddenly appear through the mist and fog and immediately strike the landing pole.

Both pilots were flung out of their cabin and died instantly. The doctors said that even though they suffered no burns, they probably died on impact. All the passengers died too. The only survivor was 22-year-old Dominique, the airhostess, and she was able to give a detailed account of what happened. She was sitting in the tail of the plane, and was strapped in alongside other passengers. Suddenly there was a jerking sensation which knocked her unconscious for a moment. When she opened her eyes she saw that the plane's wings were on fire. She knew it was important to think quickly. She shouted out to the passengers, but no-one answered: there was just silence. So she unbuckled her seat belt and crawled as far as she could until she was a little way out of the plane. She must have been in agony as she had two broken legs. Any minute now she knew that there might be a colossal explosion and that she desperately needed to get out. All of a sudden, three local women arrived on the scene and managed to pull Dominique to safety. The women were Miss Joan Egre, Mrs E.J Egre and Mrs Peggy Syvret. They dragged her to the edge of the field out of harm's way. A motorist who was driving by volunteered to take her straight to the hospital. Mrs Egre lived nearby and was the first to raise the alarm. She phoned the police, fire brigade and ambulance services at 7:10pm. Seconds later the official alarm was raised. After she was released from hospital, Dominique moved back to France to continue in her job as an airhostess. She returned to Jersey on 3rd November for further treatment and said that she was lucky and shocked to be alive as she was sitting so close to the other passengers, and would always wonder why it was just her who had survived. She visited the Weekly Post to view and select some photographs of the accident to give to her parents as a reminder of her miraculous escape from death.

One of the first people to attend the scene was Constable's Officer CL Till. He was getting ready to go out to dinner with his wife when they heard a terrible noise. Mr Till told her it was nothing to worry about and was probably just an airplane flying overhead. However he looked out of his front door to check, and to his astonishment found a field on fire. He rushed to help. Soon after, along with Constable's officer Till, there were fleets of fire appliances, and ambulances with many doctors and nurses. It was under chief officer FL Edmonston's authority that the firemen were asked to use foam spray, which brought the flames under control. All available police officers including members of the Honorary police (unpaid policemen) were in the field. Onlookers and curious members of the public were kept at a distance, because of the devastation which had occurred and the danger from an explosion and flames.

Some people had arrived at the scene before the emergency services and had tried to pull apart the wreckage to find survivors. There were none. Within minutes 11 bodies had been pulled from the rear of the plane and not one of them was alive.

The bodies were placed on stretchers and, after examination by the doctor, a blanket was placed over each body and face: a sign of death. The bodies were then moved to the side of the field until the ambulances could come to collect them. The front of the fuselage was lying upside down, so the police had to get tractors carrying hydraulic equipment to come to move it. Following this, one by one the remaining 12 bodies were extricated from the tangled wreckage.

Because there had only been one survivor of this terrible accident, the pathology laboratory at the General Hospital was turned into an information and enquiry room. It was the German Underground Hospital which revisited its past and became a temporary mortuary for the deceased. By 10.30pm the inspection of the carnage was complete and a press conference scheduled for the next morning. Discussions began on who was to blame. The Airport Controller reported that the Dakota had been on a scheduled flight from Paris, due to depart at 5.15pm but with take-off not happening until 5.32pm. The captain would have had weather notes before he took off and it was left to his discretion whether to fly or not, as the airport remained open even in fog. The airport was in radio communication with the Dakota but lost contact at around 7.10pm. He said that the area was now sealed off to members of the public and that they were waiting for the arrival of an inspector of aircraft from the Ministry of Aviation

There was no real answer as to what had happened and, once again, everyone seemed to blame the captain. Answers were needed not just for the purpose of writing an accident report, but for the families of the victims who had died. One really strange coincidence was that the landing pole, which the Dakota struck as it crashed-landed, was number 13. There's one for the' strange but true'

The only survivor was airhostess 22-year-old Dominique Sillère

The number 13 landing pole

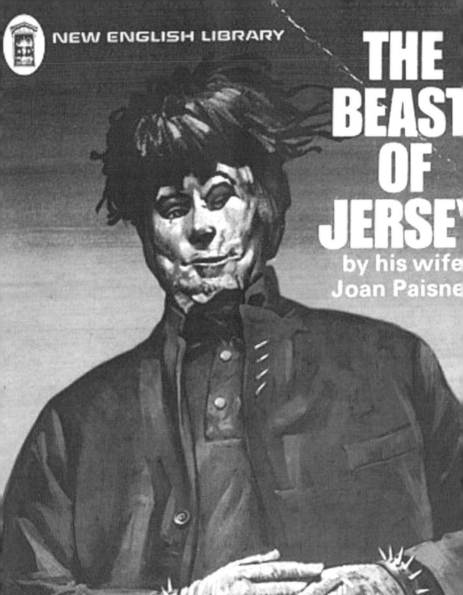

NEW ENGLISH LIBRARY

THE BEAST OF JERSEY

by his wife
Joan Paisne

Chapter Twelve

The Beast of Jersey

This story is one of the most horrific to hit Jersey. There have been books written on it, the most famous of these being by Joan Paisnel, the wife of the 'beast'. It is a tale of black magic, deluded fantasies and child sex abuse. Edward Paisnel, or Ted as he was known, was the man behind 12 years of sex crimes in the Island. For women and children, those years between 1960 and 1971 felt as if a curfew had been inflicted upon them, as it was not considered safe to be out after dark. The men of the families were known to sleep with revolvers under their pillows, waiting for an intruder to appear. Homes looked abandoned as people bolted shutters over their doors and windows. As he crept through young children's windows at night, taking them from their own beds, he seemed more like a ghost - a psychotic version of the bogey man - than a real person.

He was a man who liked to live in his own little world, a place that he could create with his fertile imagination. There were some elements to his personality that came across as being very theatrical, and he changed roles regularly. For instance, on some occasions he would alter his appearance to resemble particular movie characters: in his mind he believed he looked like them, or perhaps he wanted to become them. When Joan first met Ted she could see he was an exceptional sort of person, very good with children, if not a little odd. She felt he just needed some mothering. However his relationship with his wife would seem strange to any onlooker. He would never sit down at the table at meal-times but would sit in a corner alone. He had built separate living quarters for himself at the other end of the house, and as man and wife they had not shared the same bed for over a decade.

The house, called Maison Du Soleil, was a large one, made up of four different establishments under the same roof. It was L shaped. The main part, the vertical of the 'L', housed Ted's parents, with separate accommodation for Ted's sister and her husband. Ted, Joan and her children from her previous marriage had the horizontal of the 'L', with Ted occupying his separate office-cum-bedsit.

The victims of Ted's harrowing crimes were mainly children. Over more than a decade he committed nearly two dozen crimes against young women and children. Police investigating the crimes saw a connection between each one and believed this to be the same person but seemed powerless in catching him. The disturbing details can be emotional to read, but they need to be said to bring a sense of reality to what happened. I don't think it is fair to bring every single case back into the light and name all the children because they have suffered enough. Here is a quick run-through of the harmful and terrorising acts this man brought to our Island. Many of the children were awoken from their beds as he appeared through their windows and forced them to follow him. They were taken to dark, cold, lonely places where they were raped. Many were found with markings on their backs from his studded wrist bands and many of the younger children sustained serious physical injuries. Allegedly one girl who had been raped during that time became pregnant and bore the child of her unknown assailant. During this reign of terror, families living in what had previously seemed like quaint secluded cottages were now afraid of being too isolated, and never sure if anyone was watching them. Children were kept indoors and not encouraged to play outside. These families were missing out on a happy, safe life because of one very sick man.

People would not walk their dogs at night and were scared if they had to get a bus and then have to walk a short distance. One lady I have spoken to remembers walking down a dark country lane one night on her way home after getting off a bus from town. A man in a long dark coat suddenly appeared from behind and brushed past, he then disappeared into the darkness as her husband approached to meet her. Was that the Beast on the prowl?

In recent years a number of unsolved rape cases of young women during that time are also believed to have been committed by him. His memory lives on - in May 2006 his name cropped up again in connection with an unsolved murder from 1967 in which Tuula Hoeoek was bludgeoned to death in a field. The Police and her family are still appealing for any information as the case remains open.

On 10th July 1971, PC John Riseborough and PC Tom Mc Ginn were out patrolling St Helier in their squad-car. It was like any other night, and the most they expected from their shift was a couple of rowdy drunks, and maybe a few teenages hanging around. It was 11.45pm and they were on Route du Fort, right by the seafront. Here they waited at a red light. As they idled the engine, a small Morris 1100 saloon jumped the lights. They drove after the car and attempted to wave the man down, but didn't get his attention. They switched on their blue light but were still ignored. Now the officers switched on the klaxon, but if made no difference. It was beginning to look very suspicious. Maybe he was a drunk driver, or the car had been stolen. They speeded up and so did the Morris, roaring at 70mph through the small Jersey coastal roads. Suddenly they came to a blind alley - the man in front had taken a wrong turning. They were on a private lane when the Morris crashed through a gate and onto a footpath. It then ploughed straight through an eight-feet high hedge, landing in a tomato field. Luckily for the two police officers, there was now a gaping hole in the middle of the hedge, so they were able to follow him through. In a bigger stroke of luck they found that the Morris had come to an abrupt halt. It had been stopped by the bamboo canes supporting the tomato plants, which had rammed themselves through the front of the radiator grill and caused the engine to stall. A foot-chase started. Mc Ginn radioed headquarters informing them of their situation, while Riseborough - a keen rugby player - chased the man. After 200 yards, Riseborough was able to bring the man down in a low tackle, but he fought back with an almost satanic fury. Then the man tried his luck by saying that he had a bad heart. It was nothing that the officer hadn't heard before. When reinforcements showed up, it put a stop to any plans of escape. Riseborough and Mc Ginn, not knowing who they had caught, were more worried that their car would have to be written off. They discussed how the man they had captured would be charged with at least seven motoring offences.

In the early hours of the morning, they brought the man in and discovered something quite peculiar. He had been wearing a blue coat with inch-long, very sharp nails protruding from each shoulder. In the coat's left lapel there were also nails. He had two pieces of cloth tied around his hands. As reality hit,

Riseborough thought of the injuries he could have suffered if he had arrested the man in the normal way. On a closer inspection of the jacket the police found a spiky-haired black wig, a small silver torch covered with black tape to narrow the beam, two lengths of sash cord, a pyjama cord, woollen cap, handkerchief, watch, several empty cigarette packets and a pair of black cotton gloves. The officers informed CID. Detective Sergeant John William Marsh arrived within 10 minutes. As Marsh made a further inspection of the man now identified as Edward Paisnel, he asked him what he was doing, Ted replied quite arrogantly that he was on his way to an orgy. Inside the rubber lining of the coat Marsh found a mask and a role of adhesive tape. He now realised that this could be the sex fiend who had been causing such heartache throughout the Island. What was more worrying was that he saw adhesive marks on Paisnel's cheek,s meaning that the mask had been worn that night. Detective Inspector George Shutler arrived to take charge of the inquiries and Marsh was sent to look over the Morris 1100, which had been left in the tomato field. He found nothing incriminating in the car: just a raffia cross of the type that is given out on Palm Sunday.

While Ted was detained at the police station, officers arrived at the Paisnels' house at 2.55am. The strange layout of the house was immediately apparent: they couldn't find the front door. With no reply they had to climb up a ladder to gain entry. Once in the house they banged on doors, waking Joan and her family. She went into the hallway to discover her home was full of police officers. Straight away they asked her if she knew where her husband was, but she did not. She assumed that he had been in his separate living quarters, 20 yards from the main door. As the first search went on, the police found nothing on which they could hold Ted. They did find diaries and tapes, one of which had a harrowing story on it about a child getting pecked to death by chickens. They discovered some after-shave, that later would be used in evidence (they asked a young boy, a victim of the 'beast', to smell it: it was the same smell he remembered from his attacker). They also took away some cotton wool which had been made into an arch shape. Marsh, being so close to the case, remembered one victim's statement, in which they described the assailant as having big white eyebrows just like Father Christmas.

The next day Marsh was sure they had missed something vital to the case. At 7.30pm that night they returned to Maison Du Soleil. They searched through books, and found volumes on everything from European history, judo and hypnotism, to studies of communism. There were also plenty of books on black magic. In the corner of the room was a red curtain hung up in like a tapestry. Marsh pulled it back to discover a shallow alcove, padded with a dark carpet underfelt. Hanging inside was a large wooden dagger, a shelf with a jar of cloves, a glass chalice and a china toad. It resembled a shrine. Again Marsh remembered back in 1963 that one victim was asked to kiss a wooden object that was attached to a man's belt. He banged on the back of the alcove and it sounded hollow. Tugging on the wall the officers realised that it was like a cupboard, and noticed a keyhole. It took two men an hour and 20 minutes to get through the wall. Once inside, they saw a long fawn raincoat lined in red, an item of clothing that many victims had also described, along with a musty smell. They were afraid to go in as they did not know what to expect. When they did they found a dark blue track suit, a cloth cap and a home-made brown wig with a clipping inside from the Jersey Evening Post of 14 March 1969. There was also a pair of rubber ankle-boots and a camera. Before anything could be touched or removed for evidence, they had to wait for a police photographer. Most of the objects and walls had been painted blue, and Ted was later to reveal that this was because it is the colour of the sky and represents freedom: there is some sort of irony or hypocrisy in that, but it made sense to him. The officers also discovered a loft containing hundreds of photographs, some incriminating Ted. They now had enough evidence to charge him with much more than those seven driving offences.

On 12th July 1971, the day after the police had been back to her house, Joan went to see Ted. She was not yet convinced that he had done these awful things. When she arrived Ted was his normal cheery self, protesting his complete innocence. He was very confident that he was going to get away with it. When Joan went home she was so confused. Ted had been so reassuring that it was not him. She phoned the police pleading with them to let him go. Within 10 minutes they arrived at her house to help calm her down. The police showed her some of the pictures of the children Ted had assaulted. They also showed Joan two anonymous letters they had received over the decade of Ted's reign of terror. One was from 1960 laughing at the fact that the police had offered a reward to catch him. The other was from 1966, in which the assailant felt overly confident that he would never be caught: "I have never had much out of this life, but I intend to get everything I can now," it said. "I have always wanted to do the perfect crime." Joan's first child from her previous marriage instantly recognised the handwriting as Ted's, but police made sure they held the letter away from her so she could not make out what it said.

With all this weight of evidence, it was clear to the police that they had finally captured this monster. It had been a long wait for the families to gain justice for their children, and emotions ran high throughout the Island. On Monday 20th September 1971, Edward John Louis Paisnel, was summoned to court for his first hearing. He was presented before the Jersey Royal Court on 15 charges in connection with the sexual offences, and another seven for driving offences. Because of the nature of his case, and the strong feelings of the Islanders, he was not allowed a jury trial as he would not have stood a chance (not that he needed one.) His tribunal would be overseen by three judges who Ted Paisnel, as the accused, chose himself. The most severe charges dated back to 1960. These included sodomy, attempted sodomy, rape, attempted rape, grave and criminal assault, and indecent assault. As the assailant had been identified by the victims, the newspapers were free to publish pictures. There were photographs of Paisnel, of a dummy wearing the clothes the police had found, and also the mask and wig. On the day of the judgement, the courtroom was full and people were congregating on the stairs and outside waiting for the verdict. He was found guilty. This hideous monster was to serve 30 years' imprisonment for the hateful things he had done to those children. Paisnel's attorney called for an appeal to reduce his sentence, but the appeal was denied and Paisnel found himself on his way to Wormwood Scrubs. Thirty years does not sound very much considering the extent of his crimes against so many people. It was a huge relief for the Island: for the first time in 12 years they were safe again. Paisnel spent the end of his sentence in a high security prison on the Isle of Wight and was released on 13th July 1991 at the age of 66. He returned briefly to Jersey, amongst hostile feelings from locals, so soon went back to the Isle of Wight but was not to enjoy his freedom for long, as he died on 29th July 1994. He was refused the right to be buried in Jersey.

For me this book has been both enjoyable and disturbing to research. Many of the stories began with rumours and legends that we hear passed down from older generations. It has given me an insight into real-life emotions - desperation and sadness, but also respect, joy and miracles. These stories are part of our heritage, good or bad. All in all, I hope that they have given you a good insight into some of the Islands' biggest news events. Hopefully in time there will be a sequel to this book, with more glimpses into our Islands' past. I would like to thank all those who have assisted me in my research and writing and made this book possible.

About the author

This is Sam Bourgeois' first book and her first stepping-stone towards hopefully becoming a professional writer.

She was born in Jersey in 1986 and attended Grainville School. When she left there, she was unsure of the career she wanted to pursue, first signing up for a media studies course and then working with children.

After a few years of extensive hair-pulling, she finally found the perfect college course for her: a one-year programme at Highlands College which has opened up new horizons, as well as providing the qualifications she needed to go to university to study creative writing and philosophy.

Through her course, Sam was encouraged to find a one-day-a-week work placement. Using her initiative, she contacted Channel Island Publishing for a possible position in order to gain some experience in the industry. She submitted samples of her work and discussed various projects with them at length, following which they encouraged her to write a collection of short articles. The result of her hard work is this book being published for all to enjoy.